CREATIVE
CANVAS
EMBROIDERY

1. TREE—Wall hanging done in tent stitch. Designed by Margaret Haines Ransom, worked by Mrs. Junius Cook, Jr.

CREATIVE CANVAS EMBROIDERY

BY BUCKY KING

 *published by*

Hearthside Press, Inc.
New York

CONTENTS

CHAPTER   I   A BRIEF HISTORY OF
EMBROIDERY, 13

Embroidery in the Middle Ages, 13
English Tradition, 14
The Tudor Period, 15
The First Samplers, 15
Early Crewel Embroidery, 16
The Later Centuries, 17

CHAPTER   II   BASIC MATERIALS AND
DEFINITIONS, 18

Selecting the Canvas, 18
Preparing the Canvas, 20
Needles, 20
Threads and Yarns, 21
Some Common Misnomers, 21
Outline of Procedure for Practicing
Stitches, 22

CHAPTER   III   A VOCABULARY OF STITCHES, 23

Correcting Mistakes, 24
Flat Stitches, 24
Crossed Stitches, 38
Other Embroidery Stitches Suitable for
Canvas Work, 48

CHAPTER   IV   COLOR AND DESIGN
ON CANVAS, 51

The Basic Principles of Design, 55
Color, 62
Harmonies from Color Wheels, 62
Colors Create Mood, 66
Pointers for Working Out Color
Schemes, 67
Putting the Design on Canvas, 67
Designing with Stitches, 74
Designing with Natural Forms, 76
Impressionistic Design, 76

Adapting Designs for Use, 79
Consider the Shapes, 79
Ecclesiastical and Heraldic
    Embroidery, 81
Color and Design in Period Decoration, 84
Procedure for Canvas Embroidery, 87

CHAPTER   V   BLOCKING AND MOUNTING, 88
Blocking, 88
Mounting, 89
Joining Canvas, 92

CHAPTER   VI   PROCEDURES FOR TEACHERS
AND SUPPLIERS, 93
Recommended Requirements for
    Teachers, 94
The Classroom, 97
Classes for Children, 97
Embroidery as Therapy, 99
The Equipment, 99
Embroidery Shops, 102
Candidates for Teaching
    Accreditation, 103

CHAPTER   VII   EMBROIDERY FOR USE
AND EXHIBITION, 104
Exhibitions, 104
Judging, 106
Staging, 107
Themes, 111
Awards and Rewards, 114
Selling Entries, 115
How to be a Good Exhibitor, 115
Classifying the Exhibitors, 115

CHAPTER VIII   THE CONTEMPORARY APPROACH
TO EMBROIDERY, 118

BIBLIOGRAPHY, 121

ABOUT THE COLOR PLATES, 122

INDEX, 123

ACKNOWLEDGMENTS

Thanks are due to the many designers who permitted me to use examples of their embroidery, to my students who cooperated so generously, and to Georgiana Brown Harbison for her advice and interest. Also I should like to thank Jay Bee Studios and J. Ormsley Phillips for their assistance with the photographs.

My appreciation to Miss Alice B. Beer, Curator of Textiles at the Cooper Union Museum for the Arts of Decoration, for technical assistance, and also to Mrs. Jane Airey, who has done most of my typing.

I am deeply indebted to my husband and three sons, who patiently endured a household full of disruptions and thereby made this book possible.

I would particularly like to thank my editor, Nedda C. Anders, for her sincere interest, understanding and actual assistance in producing this book. She has contributed a great deal to its final draft, above and beyond the call of duty.

Bucky King

FOREWORD

Many books have been written for those who wish to produce fine embroidery. However, I know of no American publication which is devoted to canvas work. Now Mrs. King has written one. Drawing on her own considerable experience, she tells how to prepare the beautiful canvases which are so much in demand today. She has filled her book with working diagrams of numerous stitches and patterns, all clearly illustrated and certain to help those who are learning about this subject. Besides offering a wealth of material on techniques, Mrs. King gives an illuminating chapter on the history of canvas work. It will appeal to all who like to delve a bit past the strictly "how to do it."

Best of all are Mrs. King's suggestions for designing one's own patterns. She gives several methods for inducing imaginative compositions, including some exercises used by famous artists to create their paintings which can be most stimulating to an embroiderer. These should be of inestimable value as visual aids for teachers.

Mrs. King challenges the woman who wastes her energy filling in needlepoint backgrounds around hackneyed patterns. This book offers one of the finest explanations I have read on how to use one's own talent and energy in stitching contemporary canvases. With thoughtful planning, perhaps the reader can compose a masterpiece harmonious with the interior it graces. Who knows, in time it may become a worthy inheritance, reflective of the twentieth century and of the skill of the embroideress.

I am happy and honored to write this foreword to Mrs. King's book and feel she is to be congratulated upon a splendid contribution to the working library of all embroidery enthusiasts.

Georgiana Brown Harbeson

Bucks County
New Hope, Pa.

CREATIVE CANVAS EMBROIDERY

1

A Brief History of Embroidery

Embroidery, the art of applying ornamental needlework to a variety of materials, has existed since the earliest civilizations. It was mentioned in the Bible, examples of it were unearthed in Egyptian tombs, and it was practiced by American Indians. In fact, no civilization has ever been found in which its people did not use some type of needlework to enrich their garments and other possessions.

Canvas embroidery is stitchery worked on woven fabric, canvas or linen of varying sizes; usually the complete surface of the material is covered. It is not to be confused with real tapestry in that the latter is woven on a loom, while canvas work is always applied with a needle to a group of warp and weft threads.

EMBROIDERY IN THE MIDDLE AGES

Canvas work is one of the strongest and most durable forms of embroidery; early Coptic pieces dating from the fourth century are still in existence. Originally canvas work was called Opus Pulvinarium, meaning cushion work. In these early pieces the stitches covered the entire ground and pattern, thereby strengthening the material while ornamenting its surface. In later examples, especially during the thirteenth and fourteenth centuries, canvas work was usually done on linen with part of the ground left exposed. The softness of the material and the flatness of the stitches made the work very pliable.

ENGLISH TRADITION

A great deal of early American embroidery stems from Great Britain, so it seems only fitting to mention historical English traditions. From the mid-thirteenth to the mid-fourteenth century, English embroidery reached its highest achievement. The famous Opus Anglicanum dates from this time. Particularly notable, both in design and technique, was ecclesiastical embroidery. A fine example from this period is the orphrey, a long narrow trim on the Syon Cope (or hooded vestment) worked entirely in cross-stitch and long-armed cross on linen. Tent stitch is also shown on the cope at Pienza and chequer stitch on an English orphrey of the mid-thirteenth century at Serida in Spain. Examples of fine vestments may also be found in Rome, as the English Kings often gave rich embroideries to the Popes. This early canvas embroidery was usually silk thread, worked on even-weave linen to insure pliability. A splendid chasuble or Eucharist vestment of this era depicting the "Adoration of the Magi" may be seen at the Metropolitan Museum of Art in New York. Although most of the embroidery remaining from this interval is ecclesiastical, some domestic buskins (embroidered stockings) and sandals are still in existence. Gold and silk threads, underside couching, split stitch for faces, overly large eyes and rich textures generally characterize the embroidery of that century.

By 1350 A.D. the term Opus Anglicanum was replaced by "façon d'Angleterre." This describes a coarser style using richer fabrics such as brocades and velvets for their own appearance. Canvas strips were applied (appliquéd) to embroidery and some canvas work was of course still done, but to a lesser extent than during the Opus Anglicanum period. The Black Death in the middle of the fourteenth century caused a marked change in embroidery because many craftsmen died before passing on their craft. By the fifteenth century, except for some notable funeral palls such as the Saddlers Company Pall and the Brewers Company Pall, fine embroidery design had practically disappeared.

THE TUDOR PERIOD

Due largely to the Reformation, embroidery in the six-
teenth century placed emphasis on domestic and ceremonial
rather than ecclesiastical articles. It is in this Tudor period
that Turkey tufting was believed to have originated, to imitate the much-sought imported Turkish carpets. The six-
teenth century also saw the formation of the Worshipful
Company of Broderers, a guild for skilled craftsmen, and
the introduction of Spanish "blackwork" by Catherine of
Aragon, first wife of Henry VIII. During the reign of Elizabeth I, cushions and table carpets of excellent quality were
produced on canvas. The Bradford table carpet and Gifford
carpet, both in the Victoria and Albert Museum, London,
were worked entirely in silk and wool in tent stitch, and in-
tricately shaded. To the needlewoman of that day, embroidery was necessary not only to enrich and decorate her large
home, but to occupy her hands. Almost every young girl
received some form of training in embroidery. Elizabeth her-
self was a skillful needlewoman, though not as famous as
her rival, Mary Queen of Scots. Mary evidently had a life-
long love of the craft and produced many intricate pieces of
canvas work. Although Hardwick Hall was not completed
until after her death, Mary knew the Countess of Shrews-
bury (Bess of Hardwick), also a fine embroideress, and
Hardwick Hall contains many excellent examples of work
by these famous women.

The contemporary embroideress should take careful note
of these early pieces of canvas work, especially the interesting textures produced by the uneven qualities of the
handspun worsted thread. Much texture is lost in modern
canvas work by the craving for exactness and the use of
only one type of wool.

THE FIRST SAMPLERS

Embroidery fashions changed much more slowly in past
centuries than they do today. However, the seventeenth century brought about some notable changes. Embroidery was
used for clothes and household purposes. Needlework pic-

tures were produced purely for decoration and to show the worker's skill and knowledge in several fields of embroidery. Samplers came into being as a method of teaching young girls and as a permanent record of stitches. The earliest dated sampler, 1643, belongs in this period, although the word itself appears earlier in Shakespeare's "A Midsummer Night's Dream" (Act III, Sc. 2). Bed-furnishings, wall hangings, cut-work, clothes and upholstery were all embroidered. Stump work, a curious form of raised and padded work used to decorate small boxes, picture frames and mirrors, came into being. Though it imitated sculpture with high relief figures and animals it is quite amusing in its detail.

The Hatton Garden hangings, six in number, about seven feet by four feet, are an interesting example of canvas work. The design shows a classic column with many vines, leaves, flowers and fruit, and at least four different canvas stitches used to cover the entire work. They hang now in the Victoria and Albert Museum in London.

EARLY CREWEL EMBROIDERY

Crewel work or Jacobean work thrived during this period; the designs, formerly thought to be inspired by the newly imported Indian cotton prints, actually originated in England and were sent out to India by the East India Company trade ships, then copied on to Indian cotton palimpores. Unfortunately, twentieth century copies of this type of work have so mutilated the designs that a fake type of embroidery, with none of the originality of the early work, has resulted. Just as the needlewoman of the seventeenth century produced her own fresh ideas of fruits, flowers, birds and animals, based on her personal approach to the subject, so the contemporary worker can and should follow her own ideas, rather than copy earlier work.

American crewel had its origin in England, and though our ancestors found it necsesary to produce their own plant dyes for wools, our early patterns were quite similar to the English ones except, of course, for the American colors.

THE LATER CENTURIES

The eighteenth century brought further changes in embroidery. Samplers became framed decorations and embroidery on petticoats and aprons was abundant. Large carpets of Georgian style were produced in canvas work, and canvas embroidery was found on shoes and upholstery. Early American canvas work of this time can be seen at Mt. Vernon in a set of chair seats worked by Martha Washington. The nineteenth century saw the introduction of Berlin Wool Work, so-called because the painted canvas and harsh, analine-dyed wools were imported to England and America from Berlin. These painted canvases were most often reproductions of the Old Masters, naturalistic representations of animals and flowers, embroidered for home use as curtain tiebacks, mantel pieces, etc. With the design painted on a chart, no effort was given to creative interpretation, and it is sad today to see the number of painted canvases still available in shops and stores. Far more interesting are the little diaper patterns of the nineteenth century which can provide real inspiration to contemporary work.

Embroidery in the twentieth century can be an exciting experience for the craftsman with a skillful hand and a creative mind. Modern machinery and chemicals have produced a tremendous number of synthetic wools, nylons, silks and dacrons, both in thread and fabric textiles. Imagination and a fresh approach are required to interpret them in our own times. Contemporary embroidery reaches its peak as an art only when it is designed and worked by the same person, to reflect his imagination, as well as his stitchery knowledge and his ability to create the piece to fit the function.

Let us realize that we no longer require embroidery to fill idle hours or empty houses—twentieth century life is far too busy for that. Embroidery is having its great revival because of the wish to bring individuality and beauty to creations of our machine age. The creative contemporary embroiderer might well consider whether canvases which are stencilled at a factory, or which imitate work of an earlier era, are not directly antithetical to this wish.

2

Basic Materials and Definitions

SELECTING THE CANVAS

Canvas is a heavy cloth of flax, linen, hemp, or cotton, so woven as to form regular meshes for working with a needle. The canvases differ according to the number of holes per square inch: twenty-five or more holes to the inch for very fine work; as few as three or four holes to the inch for coarse rug canvas. As a rule, the fewer the number of holes per inch, the thicker the thread or yarn which should be used; the greater the number of holes per inch, the thinner the thread or yarn. Canvas falls into two broad classifications:

Single thread or single mesh is one thread warp and weft, suitable for all canvas stitches. The beginner finds it easier to count threads on single mesh. Figs. 1, 2 and 3 show samples of single thread mesh in three sizes.

Penelope, Double Thread or Double Mesh is two-thread warp and weft (Figs. 4, 5 and 6); it is stronger for cross-stitch (gros point). However, in contemporary work it is often desirable to use the same stitch in two different sizes. Penelope canvas has an advantage in that it can be split (pricking the double threads apart to form single holes, Fig. 7) so that one stitch may be used both large and small (Fig. 8). This effect is especially useful for faces where more detail would be desirable.

Quick-point canvas: You may see a reference to quick-point canvas. This is a double-thread type, containing 5 holes to

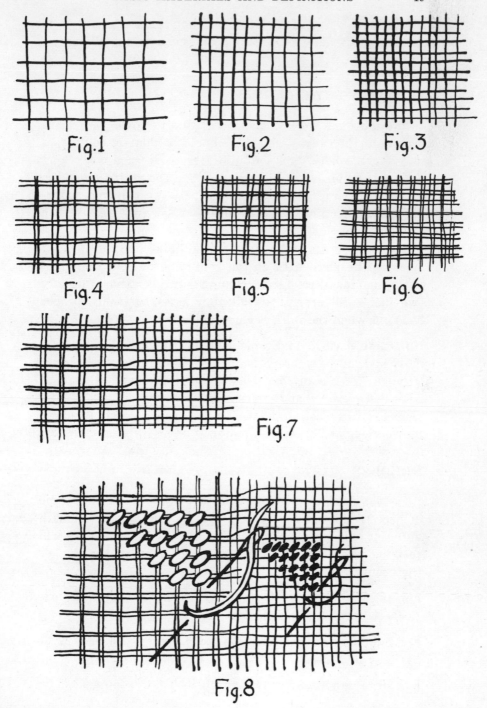

Fig.1

Fig.2

Fig.3

Fig.4

Fig.5

Fig.6

Fig.7

Fig.8

the inch; it is suited for rugs and only rugs. This term is sometimes used (erroneously) as a synonym for all canvas embroidery.

PREPARING THE CANVAS

In traditional work it was necessary to cover the entire ground of the canvas, and this should be done in contemporary work where function indicates a necessity for long wear, as in upholstery materials. When the entire ground is covered, the embroidery is stronger. However, many charming framed pictures can be worked by leaving areas of the ground open.

To work canvas embroidery in the hand, bind off all four sides of the piece with basted bias tape or seal the edges with masking tape. Leave enough surplus canvas, usually two inches all around, on all four sides to insure proper blocking when the work is completed.

No frame needed. In Europe and particularly England almost all canvas embroidery is put in a frame while being worked. After many experiments over the last 15 years, I have discovered that the frame is unnecessary, since most work must be washed and blocked when completed. Blocking instructions are given in Chapter V.

NEEDLES

Canvas needles, erroneously called tapestry needles, come in sizes 16 through 20. You will need a selection to use with different thicknesses of thread. Numbers 16, 18 and 20 will cover your basic needs. The larger the number, the smaller the needle.

For quick point and turkey tufting on rugs—the largest size 13 Boye "tapestry" needles are useful.

For fine work on fine canvas—special small needles (22 or 24) may be ordered.

For large upholstery work—number 17 is recommended.

For advanced embroidery—English needles are favored because of their smooth eyes and tempered steel.

THREADS AND YARNS

Today's synthetics provide the contemporary needle-woman with a wealth of threads, yarns and materials for canvas work.

Tapestry wools—are excellent for the coarser canvases.

Knitting yarns—especially of wool and nylon, are very good because they come in many different tones and colors.

Persian yarns—sold in some of the finer needlework supply shops, the best of all the wools, since they come in many graded shades and can be made thicker or thinner because of the three-ply separate mercerized construction.

Filoselle and Filofloss—mercerized silks and cotton embroidery floss, add luster and highlights.

Nylon sock-and-sweater yarn—also good for covering backgrounds of articles that will see hard use, since this yarn resists dirt.

Raffia and some of the soft cotton strings add interest and texture. The thickness of the threads is always governed by the stitch used (some require thicker threads, some thinner), and the size of the canvas. It is advisable to select at least two different kinds of thread to add texture and interest to your piece. Often two strands of different color used together will create an interesting effect.

Other materials—it's fun to experiment with different possibilities. I have seen lovely examples of work done with dental floss, heavy rug yarn and rope, worked on burlap.

SOME COMMON MISNOMERS

Needlepoint—a type of lace made entirely with a needle on a parchment or paper pattern. Also the name of an embroidery stitch, it should not be used as a synonym for canvas work.

Gros point—a type of Venetian point distinguished by raised work and large stitch. Sometimes misused to describe canvas work made with cross-stitch, Aubusson stitch or tapestry (Gobelin) stitch.

Tapestry—a heavy woven textile in which the design is usually figured and reversible, used as wall hanging, carpet or upholstery material. The design may be printed on the thread before the fabric is woven. Certain stitches useful on canvas, notably Gobelin, were intended to imitate tapestry. This led to the erroneous use of tapestry as a synonym for canvas.

OUTLINE OF PROCEDURE FOR PRACTICING STITCHES (A SAMPLER)

Placing the design on the canvas is dealt with in detail in Chapter IV. However, one needs only a blank canvas to begin a sampler, and this is often the best way to master a variety or stitches.

1) Select a variety of threads and a piece of canvas.

2) With a pencil, divide the canvas into small squares about two inches each.

3) Begin working each stitch following the directions and order given in Chapter III. Allow one square for each type of stitch, repeating each stitch as often as necessary to fill the square.

3

A Vocabulary of Stitches

Many different stitches can be embroidered on canvas, but some are better for this purpose than others. This chapter covers those which you are most likely to use in counted thread and canvas work. For easy reference it seems advisable to divide them into three groups: flat stitches, crossed stitches and a third group of stitches of limited use but effective for special purposes. The stitches are listed in their order of importance.

All stitches described are executed in the traditional way or over a given count of threads; therefore, it is unnecessary to have any knots on the reverse side of the piece.

1. To begin a blank piece of canvas, leave about one inch of thread at the back of the work. (Except in turkey knot and surrey stitch.) Hold the thread carefully in place with the fingers and stitch over from the front with the first stitch given.

2. Begin subsequent threads by weaving them through about 1½ inches of work already completed on the back. A good length for all threads is approximately 20 inches.

3. When a thread has been worked on the surface down to four inches, take it through the material to the back and weave it through work already finished. Cut off long tails of threads with a scissors to prevent them from becoming entangled in new work.

CORRECTING MISTAKES

It is easy to correct a mistake in the stitch made by missing the correct count over the threads. Repair it by plucking out the yarn with the blunt end of the needle. Since no knots have been used, this is a relatively simple operation, but it does require care and exactness.

FLAT STITCHES

No. 1 Tent is the first of the flat stitches. Often called needlepoint or, when used diagonally, petit point, it has four variations and is easily one of the best canvas stitches for all intricate work and shading.

Straight Tent Stitch, Fig. 9, is actually a half cross-stitch. Work it over one thread vertically and horizontally in rows, straight across the canvas. Do not work it in large areas as it tends to pull the material out of shape.

Trame, Fig. 10, is also a half cross-stitch worked over a laid thread on the canvas. Some prepared trame pieces are available in the needlework shops with the colored threads laid in rows on the canvas indicating the color yarn to be used for covering them.

Reverse Tent, Fig. 11, is exactly like straight tent except that the direction of the tent stitch is changed in every other row. It is excellent for indicating textures.

Diagonal Tent or Petit Point, Fig. 12, is worked over one horizontal and one vertical thread but on the diagonal across the canvas. It forms a pronounced basket-weave pattern on the reverse side and will not pull the canvas out of shape. It is also much stronger and longer wearing than the other tent stitches and should be used for all large areas, and especially rugs and upholstery. Tent stitches will produce naturalistic forms or any forms which require intricate shading.

Gobelin is the canvas stitch which imitates the tapestry from which it takes its name. It forms pronounced ridges in the ground very similar to those in woven tapestries, and

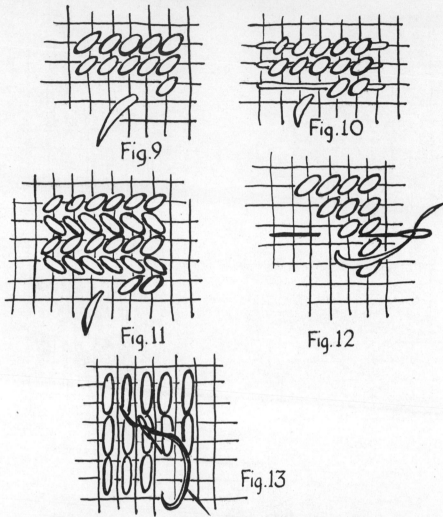

Fig.9

Fig.10

Fig.11

Fig.12

Fig.13

can be worked over 2, 3, 4 or more horizontal threads. Since it will cover the ground more rapidly than tent, as well as provide a contrasting texture, it is very good for backgrounds. Shading can be accomplished nicely in Gobelin Droit, Oblique, and Encroaching.

Gobelin Droit (straight), Fig. 13, is worked in horizontal rows over 2, 3, 4 or more horizontal threads. Gobelin Droit, Oblique and Encroaching will produce a tapestry-like appearance when used for an entire piece.

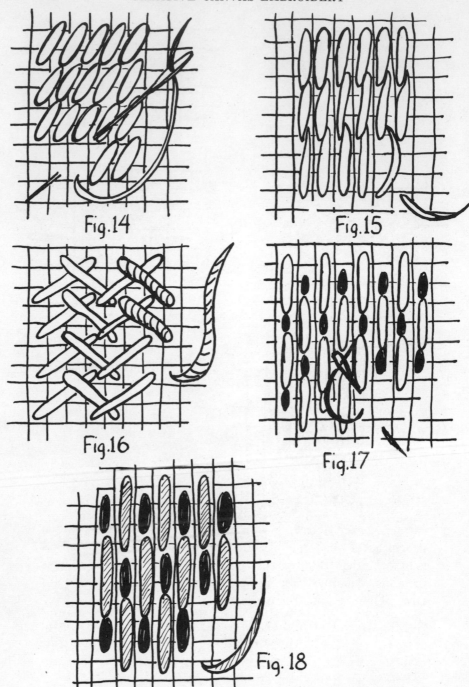

Fig.14

Fig.15

Fig.16

Fig.17

Fig. 18

Gobelin Oblique (slanting), Fig. 14, is worked in horizontal rows over 2, 3, 4 or more horizontal threads and one thread vertically.

Gobelin Encroaching, Fig. 15, is worked in horizontal rows over 2, 3, 4 or more horizontal threads, either droit or oblique, and one thread vertically, encroaching over one thread of the previous row.

Gobelin Plait, Fig. 16 (described on page 43), is worked in vertical rows and, since it is actually a cross-stitch, in two parts. However, it is mentioned here because it belongs to the family of Gobelin stitches.

Parisian Stitch, Fig. 17, is worked in horizontal rows and can be shaded in solid colors or an alternate color can be used for the short stitch. The stitch can be worked two ways both in size and color, Fig. 18. It can be worked over one and three threads horizontally or two and four threads horizontally. The long stitch always comes directly under the short stitch.

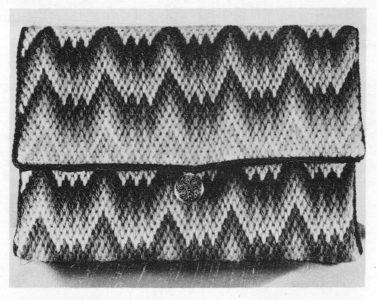

2. PURSE—Done in Florentine stitch and pattern. Designed and worked by Jane Burrows.

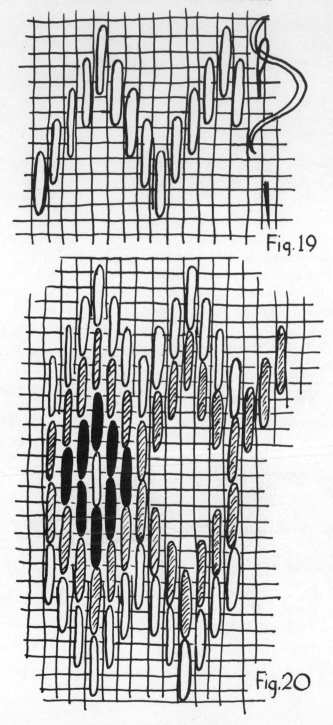

Fig. 19

Fig. 20

Florentine Stitch also called Flame or Bargello work, Fig. 19, originated in Florence where it was thought to have been introduced by a Hungarian who married into the Medici family. It is much used for upholstery, either in silk or wool. The bases for most of the traditional repeat patterns are peaked triangles or graded shades, usually not more than two hues but four to six tones of each, Fig. 20. These triangular peaks of shaded color have caused the stitch to be called "flame," and even to be considered as a separate type of embroidery because of the many patterns possible in both traditional and contemporary work.

Florentine stitch is most often worked over an even number of horizontal threads, usually four or six, and moves upwards or downwards to produce the "flame" spikes. The basic peaked pattern and several others are illustrated, but the possibilities are numerous. The stitch will produce any peaked and shaded pattern, including the scales on a fish.

Hungarian Stitch or Point d'Hungrie, Fig. 21, is worked in units over two, four, and two horizontal threads, leaving two vertical threads between each unit, before repeating the three stitches. The second row always interlocks the first,

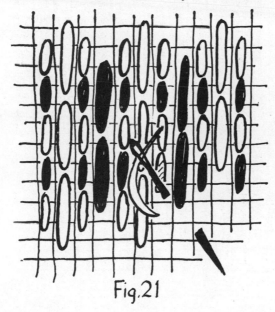

Fig. 21

with the little stitches coming under the little stitches and the large stitches coming between them. It is effective either in solid color or two colors using either wool or silk or a combination of one silk row with one wool row.

Hungarian Ground Stitch, Fig. 22, is actually more closely related to Florentine work than Hungarian stitch, but bears this name because the center diamond may be filled with either small upright Gobelin stitches or Hungarian stitch. It is worked in zigzag rows over four horizontal threads to form center diamonds which are filled with four upright Gobelin stitches over two horizontal threads. Large areas worked in this stitch are very effective and again the contrast of wool, silk, or cotton, used together, produces interesting highlights.

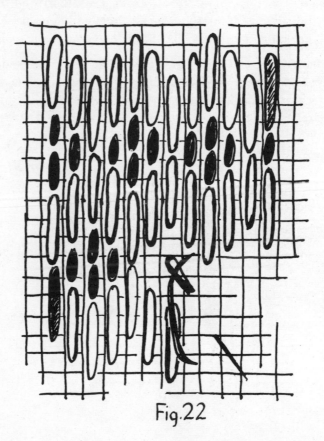

Fig. 22

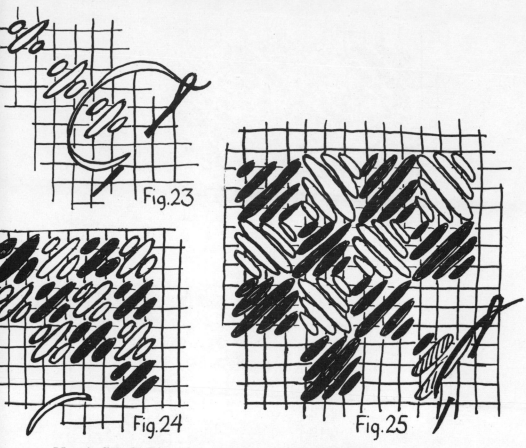

Fig. 23

Fig. 24

Fig. 25

Mosaic Stitch, Fig. 23, is closely related to Hungarian stitch, but is worked in diagonal rows in units of three; first over one horizontal and one vertical thread, next over two horizontal and two vertical threads, and finally over one horizontal and one vertical thread. In essence each unit consists of one tent stitch, one slanting Gobelin, and one tent stitch. The combination of threads and alternating colors in the diagonal rows add interest, Fig. 24.

Flat Stitch, Fig. 25, is actually a form of mosaic stitch and is worked in diagonal rows in opposite directions, over one, two, three, two and one threads, vertically and horizontally on the canvas. When worked in large areas it gives a quilted effect and covers the canvas best in wool.

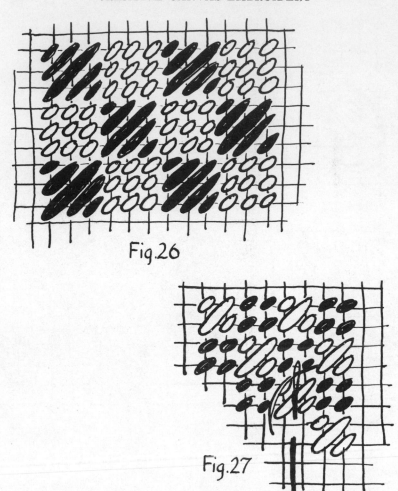

Fig. 26

Fig. 27

Chequer Stitch, Fig. 26, is a combination of two stitches, tent and flat. The squares of flat stitch are worked in diagonal rows, over one, two, three, two, and one threads. The remaining squares are filled in with tent stitch.

Small Chequer Stitch, Fig. 27, is also a combination of two stitches, mosaic and tent. Work the mosaic stitch in diagonal lines over one, two and one threads. Then work four tent stitches, forming a square of the same size; finally repeat the diagonal line of mosaic stitch.

Scotch Stitch, Fig. 28, is another combination of tent and flat stitch, in which the squares of flat stitch are worked diagonally over one, two, three, two and one threads skipping one vertical and one horizontal thread between the working of each diagonal square. Fill in the thread between the squares with one row, all around, of tent stitch.

Moorish Stitch, Fig. 29, is worked diagonally, very like flat stitch, except that the small stitch over one vertical and one horizontal thread forms the corner of both squares. The stitch runs diagonally over one, two, three, and two threads vertically and horizontally. Use tent stitch to fill in the lines between rows.

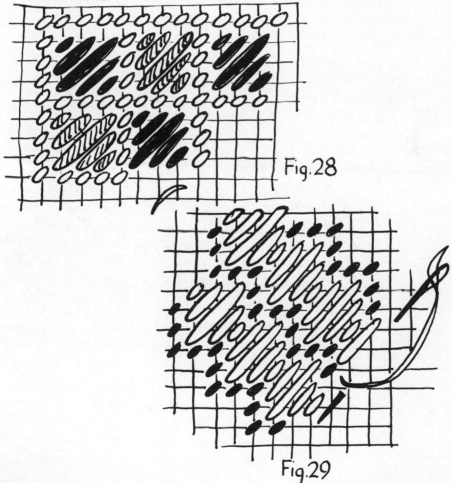

Fig. 28

Fig. 29

Oriental Stitch, Fig. 30, is worked diagonally in units of four over one, two, three, and four threads, vertically and horizontally, forming small triangles. It may be worked solidly or together with Gobelin oblique filling in the empty spaces.

Jacquard Stitch, Fig. 31, is actually a diaper pattern of tent and Gobelin oblique. Work it diagonally over two vertical threads and two horizontal threads over a count of five stitches on the horizontal plane and five down on the vertical. Use tent stitch before repeating another row.

Byzantine Stitch, Fig. 32, is very similar to jacquard stitch except that the row of tent stitches is omitted. It is effective for graduating the shades of one color.

Knitting Stitch, Fig. 33, is worked on Penelope canvas in vertical rows, over two double horizontal threads, and between one pair of vertical threads. It is an interesting stitch for rugs and will produce an effect similar to knitting when used in large areas.

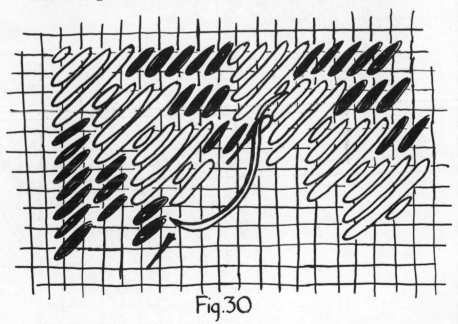

Fig. 30

The Leopard

RESTAURANT

ON TO 2:30 • 6:30 TO 11:00

EAST 50TH STREET, RESERVATIONS ONLY, PL 9-3735

very different from … sp…
sense that the former implies p…
Older people work things out …
tems passively by going to spe…
say, the cinema. There they c…
iously everything that is forbi…
life. Hence the eroticism and …
so many films, which compens…
frustrations.

But in all this modern man …
sive. He looks, but he doesn't …
our civilization of frenzy can a…
a civilization of apathy. The fee…
apathetic and we even react …
a road accident: we look and …
And take the Carnival at Nice …
are the passive spectators wh…
other side are the paid clown…
come a mere spectacle, and i…
fete in which everyone partici…

As for the masses—the wo…
for example—they have only …
ship behind and begun to …
material conditions. From t…
view, the technological socie…
advantages. Why should the…
we have just started to enjo…
into question? Today's work…
over to the other side of t…
It's the young who feel alien…

*There is another striking ch…
this third culture. In the p…
culture of the privileged cla…
international. The lower one…
social scale, the more cu…
provincial and particularize…
have a new popular culture …
mediately become a mass …*

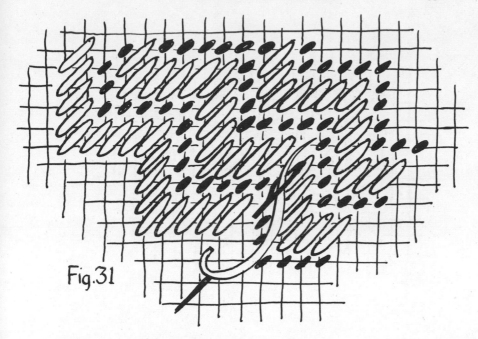

Fig. 31

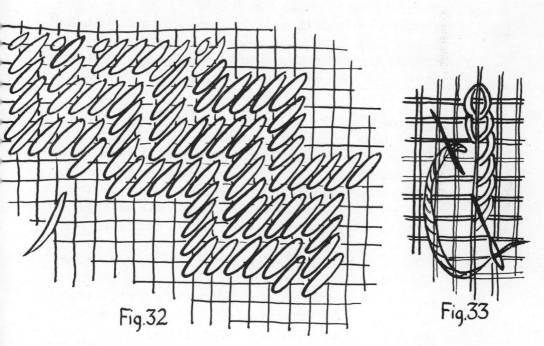

Fig. 32

Fig. 33

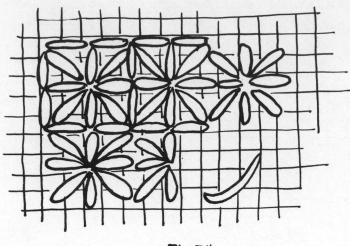

Fig. 34

Star Stitch or Algerian Eye Stitch, Fig. 34, is a square stitch worked in units over two threads, the unit consisting of four threads per unit. The needle must always go down through the center hole, making eight stitches over two threads per unit. Back stitch may be worked around the edges, should the canvas show through.

Diamond Eyelet Stitch, Fig. 35, is also worked in units, sixteen stitches per unit, with the needle always going down through the center hole. The stitches forming the points of the diamond are worked over four threads; the intervening stitches over three, then two, then three and the point over four threads. Back stitch can be worked around the outside if the canvas shows. This stitch produces small holes when worked in large areas.

Two diaper patterns are also given, Figs. 36 and 37, indicating the limitless possibilities in combining the stitches to produce different effects. Many other ideas can be obtained by looking at the patterns on woven fabrics, from which this term "diaper patterns" originated.

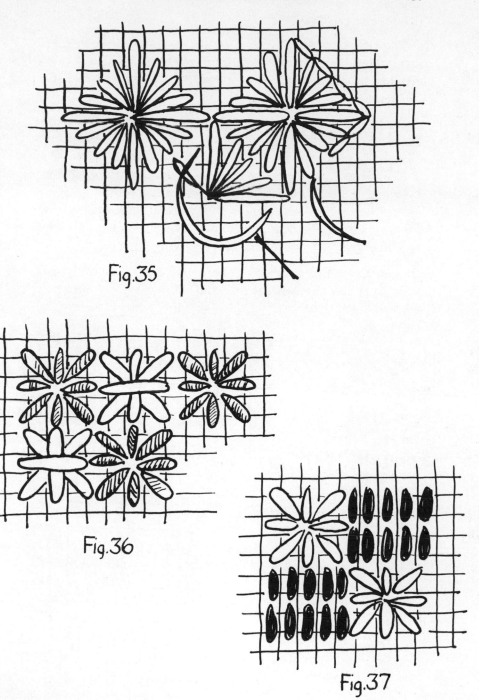

Fig. 35

Fig. 36

Fig. 37

CROSSED STITCHES

The second division of canvas stitches are those that are interlocked, crossed over, knotted, or tufted. Many of these stitches require considerably more thread or yarn to cover the canvas.

Cross-Stitch or Gros Point, Figs. 38, 39, is worked in two different ways; either as a single unit, working one row of half cross-stitch and working over this row, coming back with the crossing stitch or, more usual, worked in horizontal rows over one or two threads vertically and horizontally, crossing each stitch separately. When it is worked over one thread, its completed appearance very much resembles diagonal tent on the surface. It is excellent for shading, Fig. 40.

Oblong Cross-Stitch, Fig. 41, is worked in horizontal rows over varying number of threads. The diagram shows it worked over two vertical threads and four horizontal threads.

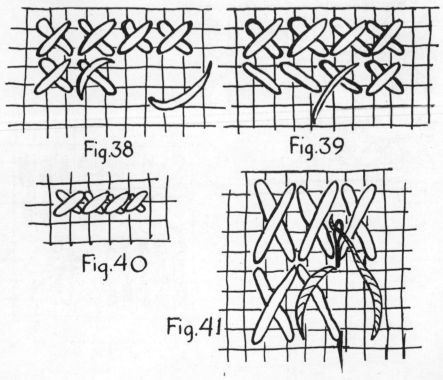

Fig. 38   Fig. 39

Fig. 40

Fig. 41

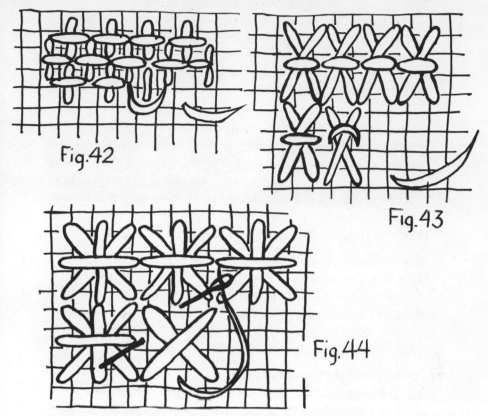

Fig. 42

Fig. 43

Fig. 44

Straight Cross, Fig. 42, is worked in interlocking horizontal rows over two vertical threads and two horizontal threads. It is always crossed horizontally and can be shaded effectively. It will produce a tight, strong and bumpy surface, excellent for roads, flower centers, trees and beaches.

Oblong Cross-Stitch with Back Stitch, Fig. 43, is worked in horizontal rows over two vertical and four horizontal threads with the back stitch over two threads directly in the center. Each unit is completed before going on with the next stitch, using one color.

Smyrna Cross or Double Cross, Fig. 44, is worked in horizontal rows over four threads vertically and horizontally. The large cross is completed first and the straight cross worked over it. Two colors may be used for striking effect.

Large Cross and Straight Cross, Fig. 45, is a composite stitch in which the large cross is worked first over four threads vertically and horizontally and the straight cross is fitted into the remaining space, covering two threads vertically and horizontally. Again, two colors make an interesting contrast.

Double Stitch, Fig. 46, is a composite stitch, worked in varying number of threads, in which the oblong cross is worked first over two vertical and six horizontal threads. The oblong crosses interlock, and cross-stitch is worked in between over two vertical and horizontal threads. If only one color is used it may be worked in rows beginning with the oblong cross then working the cross and repeating the oblong cross.

Rice Stitch or Crossed Corners Stitch, Fig. 47, is a composite stitch usually worked in wool for the large cross and silk or cotton for the crossed corners. It is worked in horizontal rows, the large cross over four threads vertically and horizontally and the arms of the cross over two threads vertically and horizontally, and usually in two colors.

Double Straight Cross-Stitch, Fig. 48, is worked in interlocking horizontal rows, the large straight cross over four threads vertically and horizontally held down by a cross-stitch over two threads vertically and horizontally, so that the stitches interlock each unit.

Stem Stitch, Fig. 49, can be worked over any number of threads. The diagram is worked over two vertically and horizontally, with the next row going in the opposite direction and filled in with back stitch. It is actually slanted Gobelin with back stitch; the rows going in opposite directions.

Fern Stitch, Fig. 50, is worked in vertical rows over four threads vertically and horizontally at its broad point and two threads vertically and horizontally at its narrow point, skipping two horizontal threads between each stitch. The needle comes up at (1) goes in at (2), out at (3) in at (4) and is ready to begin again at (1). It will produce a braided effect.

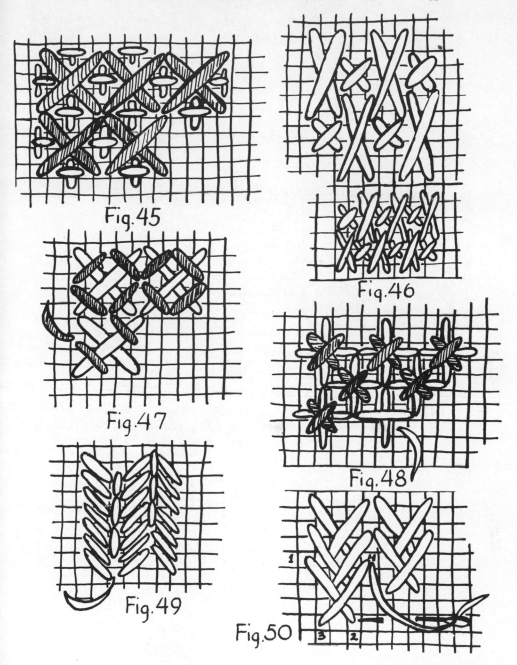

Fig. 45

Fig. 46

Fig. 47

Fig. 48

Fig. 49

Fig. 50

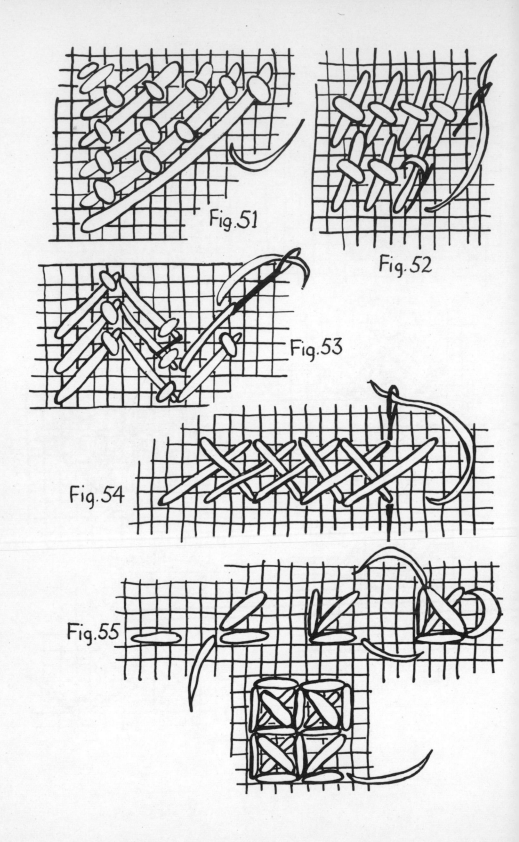

Fig. 51

Fig. 52

Fig. 53

Fig. 54

Fig. 55

Web Stitch, Fig. 51, is worked diagonally from left to right by laying one diagonal thread at a time and couching it down with a tent stitch, skipping one thread between each laid thread. It is very similar to Bokhara couching, except that it is always worked on the diagonal.

Knotted Stitch, Fig. 52, is worked in horizontal encroaching rows over five horizontal and two vertical threads, tied down with a crossed stitch over one horizontal and two vertical threads. The next row encroaches over one thread of the upper row.

Fishbone Stitch, Fig. 53, is worked in vertical rows over any number of threads. In the diagram it is worked over four threads vertically and horizontally and tied down with a tent stitch, each row going in opposite directions.

Gobelin Plait is worked in vertical rows over any number of threads. In the diagram it is worked over two horizontal and three vertical threads skipping two horizontal threads between each stitch. The next row is worked in the opposite direction and the stitches crossed over the first row. (See Fig. 16.)

Long-Legged Cross-Stitch, Fig. 54, is worked in horizontal rows over any number of threads. In the diagram the first stitch is worked over six vertical threads and four horizontal threads, the next stitch is crossed over the first and is worked over four horizontal and three vertical threads.

Italian Cross-Stitch, Fig. 55, is worked in units and then horizontal rows. The first stitch is worked over three vertical threads. Stitch two is worked over three vertical and horizontal threads. Stitch three is worked over three horizontal threads. Stitch four is crossed over stitch two. Stitch five is worked over three horizontal threads and stitch six over three vertical threads. In the next unit stitch three is already worked, and in the next row stitch six is already worked.

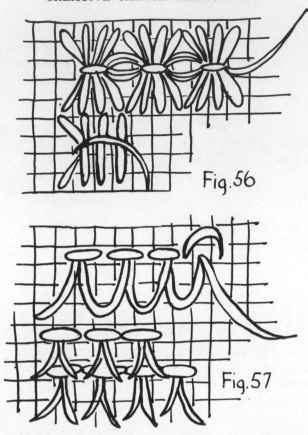

Fig. 56

Fig. 57

Shell Stitch, Fig. 56, is worked in units of four and in horizontal rows over four horizontal threads and tied down in the center with one stitch, crossing one vertical thread. Thinner thread of silk or cotton can then be passed through the tie stitch to cover the canvas or straight cross worked between each unit.

Turkey Knot Tufting, Fig. 57. Always begin this stitch from the front of the canvas and always work from the bottom up. Put the needle through a hole in the canvas and hold the tail of yarn with your thumb. Bring the needle up one thread to the left, cross two threads, bring the needle out the same hole it went in to begin, and pull tight. After each stitch, hold the loop with your thumb until the stitch has been

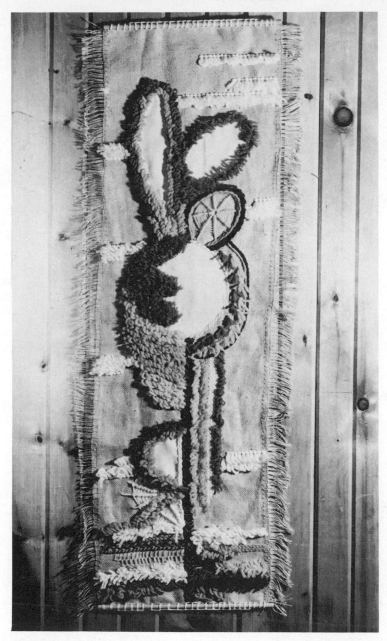

3. GROWING—Wall hanging on jute canvas with fringed sides; appliqué and Turkey knot stitches. Designed and worked by Author.

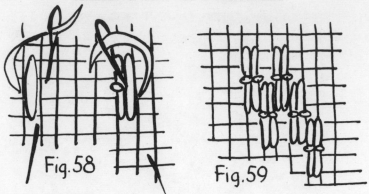

Fig. 58   Fig. 59

pulled tight. The loops may be cut, if desired for tufting. Thick knitting yarn fluffs out nicely with this stitch and it can be beautifully shaded. It will produce beautiful fur on animals and is excellent for rugs.

French Stitch, Figs. 58, 59. Care must be taken in selecting the proper thickness of yarn to work this stitch. Single thread Persian or crewel works well for ten to fourteen holes per inch. Since the yarn must enter the same unit hole twice, it should not be so thick as to change the character of the stitch.

The stitch is worked diagonally over four threads and five holes, using two stitches per unit in the same hole. One stitch is tied over the left vertical thread and the second tie stitch over the right vertical thread, using the center hole as the top thread in the next diagonal unit.

Rococo Stitch, Figs. 60, a b c d e. In order to work this stitch on canvas other than Penelope canvas, five holes to the inch, it is necessary to make a cross cut on the canvas, cutting every other thread vertically and horizontally, and withdrawing the cut threads.

Single thread Persian or crewel wool will work well, but care must be taken that the yarn used is neither too thick nor too thin. The stitch produces small holes in a repeat pattern and is worked diagonally. In principal, it is much like Roumanian stitch on fabric and once the threads are withdrawn they can be interwoven into the remaining mesh or anchored with tiny back stitches to be covered later with other stitches.

Rococo stitch is worked diagonally over units of two horizontal threads, four stitches usually filling one unit. The tie stitch on the right passes over the right vertical thread and the tie stitch on the left over the left vertical thread. It is helpful, in working, to keep the thread pulled taut.

Cutting canvas for rococo stitch, Fig. 61. To work this stitch on canvas other than Penelope, draw a Greek cross on the mesh in pencil and begin to cut every other thread, vertically and horizontally. With the blunt end of a needle, pull the threads back and weave them into the remaining mesh. This produces a larger mesh in the pulled area, thus making it possible to work rococo stitch on any size canvas.

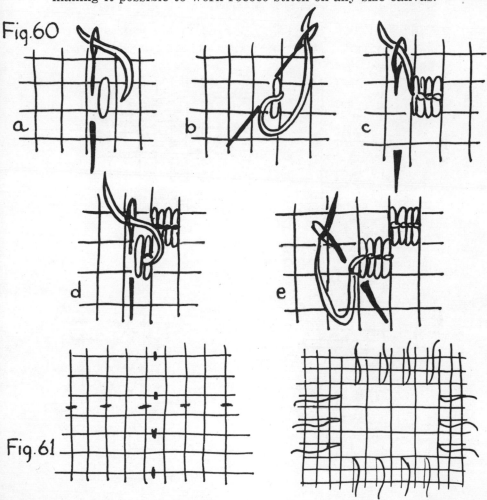

Fig. 60

a

b

c

d

e

Fig. 61

OTHER EMBROIDERY STITCHES SUITABLE FOR CANVAS WORK

Chain Stitch, Fig. 62, can be worked over any number of threads. In the diagram it is worked over two horizontal threads.

Back Stitch, Fig. 63, can be worked over any number of vertical or horizontal threads and is always excellent for filling in where canvas shows.

Bokhara Couching, Fig. 64, can be worked over any number of threads and is couched down with small upright Gobelin stitches to form different patterns.

Vandyke Stitch, Fig. 65, is worked in vertical rows over three horizontal and two vertical threads and produces a tight braid effect.

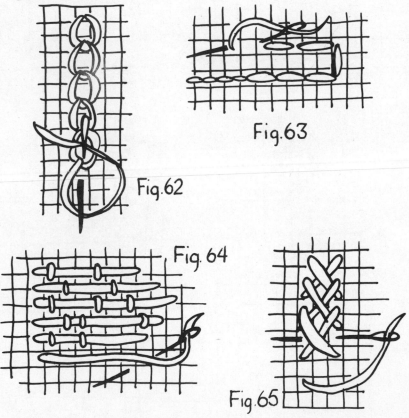

Fig.62

Fig.63

Fig. 64

Fig.65

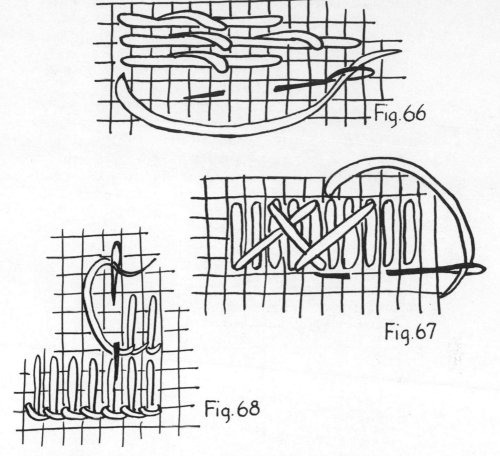

Fig. 66

Fig. 67

Fig. 68

Roumanian Couching, Fig. 66, can also be worked over any number of vertical threads. The couching stitch is always over three vertical threads, diagonally. Long rows may require four or five couching stitches.

Herringbone Couching, Fig. 67, is worked over upright Gobelin (over three, four, five, or six threads). Any count may be used for the herringbone. The diagram shows it over three vertical and horizontal threads.

Buttonhole (closed) Stitch, Fig. 68, may be worked over any count on canvas. The diagram shows it over two horizontal threads.

Pattern darning, originally used for white work, and worked with a running stitch over various threads and counts, offers limitless possibilities in canvas work.

Drawing **a** shows a simple darning thread used horizontally over a count of two threads, with tent stitch worked over the exposed thread, forming a laid pattern.

Drawing **b** shows a darning stitch worked first horizontally, over two threads skipping one thread, and then worked vertically, three stitches to the unit over two threads.

Drawing **c.** Many simple patterns may be invented, but keep in mind that the reverse side of the canvas is not well covered, and therefore as a long-wearing stitch, pattern darning has its limitations.

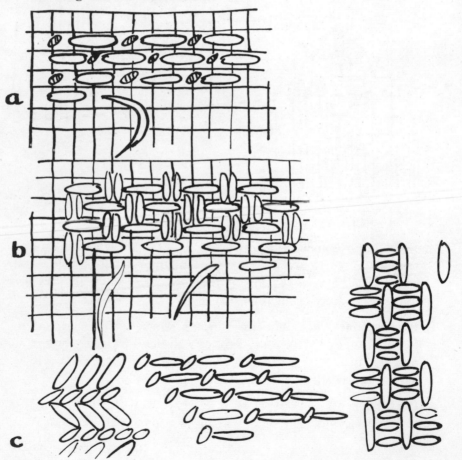

Color and Design on Canvas

How inconceivable to the needleworker of a century or two ago would have been the pre-worked canvases which are so popular today! For that matter, how unappealing they are to the discriminating contemporary embroiderer, not only because the designs are usually tasteless, but also because they leave no space for imagination, the yarns, colors and stitches, as well as the design itself, having been preselected by the manufacturer. Among the exceptions are the lovely one-of-a-kind or limited-production canvases planned by creative designers to be stitched in by their customers, but designs of this type are costly. Quite apart from the expense involved, there is far more satisfaction in seeing the product of your own imagination come to life on canvas. To keep embroidery from becoming a mechanical skill only, organizations like American Craftsman Council with affiliated groups throughout the country encourage needlewomen to design their own work.

Many would like to do so but make the excuse "I cannot draw a straight line." It happens that ability to draw is unnecessary, because canvas conceals likeness to the model. In other words, it is impossible in the limits of the material to copy natural forms with complete fidelity. Far more important than the hand trained to draw is the eye accustomed to **seeing,** an eye which can eliminate unnecessary detail and select and interpret the essential character of the subject to be represented. With such an eye and a knowledge of basic design principles, you are able to do creative embroidery.

The squared nature of the canvas will modify designs.

4. ST. MICHAEL—A wall hanging embroidered in silk, wool, and gold thread. Stitches: Gobelin, Parisian, Florentine, tent, mosaic, with gold thread couching wings. Designed and worked by Author.

THE BASIC PRINCIPLES OF DESIGN

Artists down through the ages have tried to understand the what, why and how of man-made beauty. These theorists have observed that all good designs have several common characteristics, based on nature's own rules. By more or less universal agreement, the characteristics or principles of good design have been defined as follows:

Unity: The design must be completely integrated with individual parts so arranged as to form one perfect whole.

Organic unity is achieved by creating a center of interest or focus to which all the lines of the design are directed. At this area should go the most vibrant colors, the most forceful shapes, the most compelling stitches, with all other elements subordinated. This center of interest is generally created at the points where the major lines of the design intersect. Unity may be achieved psychologically as well as organically. In Plate 5, for example, the mind records the fact that magazine covers are the unifying theme of the canvas. On further analysis, it becomes clear that all the elements of the design are no doubt related to the "time, life and fortune" of Marcia Davenport, who executed it. Note the pencils, the titles of the books she wrote, and other psychologically unified symbols. In Plate 4, note how all the lines carry the eye into the center of interest, the face of St. Michael. To support the importance of this area, note that the strongest contrasts of black and white are used here; the heaviest stitches surround it; the most forceful line of the cross leads to it. This is organic unity.

illustration opposite:
5. TIME, LIFE, FORTUNE—Desk top, all tent stitch. Worked by writer Marcia Davenport, designed by Alice Morgan Carson.

Scale and proportion: These refer to the size relationships which exist between the separate units of the design—to themselves, to the over-all plan, and to the background or frame around it; a design too small for the canvas makes as absurd an effect as one pea on a dinner plate.

Plate 1 is a good example of pleasing scale and proportion. The root and trunk, the branches and leaves, the fruits and birds, all seem to be relatively right for each other. That is, although each of the units are drawn smaller than actual size, their relative size is true to real life.

Dominance: It is a fundamental of composition that one idea, tone, color, line, texture or other element must outweigh—be more important than—the other.

In Plate 6, the triangular form is most important. The circles and rectangles are subordinated. The line direction is

6. RAISED 3-D FISH—Stitches used: Florentine, plaited Gobelin, Gobelin droit, Hungarian, Parisian, encroaching Gobelin, Hungarian ground, chain, detached stem, long and short, stem spider web. Wool. Designed and worked by Author.

A sketch indicating stitches to be used.

predominantly diagonal, well suited to express darting fish since in nature the diagonal expresses movement (as in zig-zag lightning, waves dashing against rocks, etc.). Verticals and horizontals offer needed contrast to the diagonals.

Rhythm: A good composition carries the eye through it in a certain rhythm, now held (at the center of interest), now released (by the voids or spaces). That is, the lines and shapes, the textures and colors, the spaces and masses—all of these ingredients should be used in a pleasing graduation of sizes and colors from one place to another. The eye is attracted by similar objects, similar colors, similar shapes, similar textures (and in our medium, similar stitches) so their repetition throughout the design is an important aspect of rhythm.

Plate 7 is an interesting study in rhythm. Although there is a great deal going on in this composition, the rhythmic repetition of elements interests and attracts the eye, and helps it to see the many separate parts as one unified whole. Look at the recurring (but varied) V-shapes: in the branches which divide from a common stem at the right, in the stance of the storks in the lower center, in the open beaks of the fledgling birds at the left, in the tails and wings of the birds in flight across the mid-center, and even in the veining of the leaves.

Contrast or variety: The eye is quickly sated—it becomes bored by identical, unvarying repetition. So without violating the principle of dominance, good composition skillfully introduces contrast in all the elements, so placed that their differences become emphasized. Light values play against dark, vertical lines against horizontal ones, dull yarn against bright, flat stitches against textured ones, thick against thin. Even the voids or spaces in the design are contrasted against each other.

Plate 8 exemplifies this point. Had the designer used identical lines to screen the tiger in the background, monotony would have resulted. By playing many variations on the

7. DEEP SOUTH—An all tent stitch panel measuring 72″ x 64″.
Designed and worked by Georgiana Brown Harbeson, collection
of James Lees and Sons.

8. ANOTHER TIGER—Stool top, all tent stitch. Designed by Janet Shook.

theme of verticals, interest is sustained as the viewer follows the design from the face of the tiger across the lines to the tail—which curves to impel the eye into the design—across the body, to the bars at left and back again to the tiger face. The result is a varied and aesthetically pleasurable experience.

Balance is another principle. This one too is easily observed, for man by instinct finds the stance which will give him equilibrium. There are two basic kinds of stability or balance. **In symmetrical balance,** a real or imagined line (axis) divides the composition into two halves of similar weight or force. Plate 25 is an excellent example. The two crosses (top and bottom) show where the design could be divided, down a central axis, to form two identical units. **In asymmetrical balance,** there is no division into identical or similar groups;

the objects are balanced by placement. To understand this, think of a see-saw holding two children of unequal weight. The heavier child must sit closer to the center, to balance the lighter child at the edge.

In striving for balance in design, keep the largest, brightest, most compelling masses, stitches and colors near the axis, the lighter, paler ones at the outer extremities of the composition.

9. BENCH COVER—Stitches include: tent, Gobelin, knotted cross, rice, Hungarian, buttonhole, Florentine, mosaic, flat and Turkey tufting on lamb. Wool. Designed and worked by student, Mrs. Malcom Priest.

COLOR

One man's concord may be another man's discord! In the past, pink, red, and orange were considered clashing hues, but Matisse proved that they can combine in a beautiful harmony. Since no one can be didactic about color schemes, it is important for the needleworker to consider her own tastes, as well as the purpose and eventual placement of the article to be embroidered. This little section, while not a complete treatise on color, will, I hope, enable you to make your selection with confidence in your own judgment. We start with a few definitions.

Hue: The family to which a color belongs. The color wheels which follow show twelve different hues.

Value: Describes the color in relation to light and dark. Pale pink is a light value of red. Maroon is a dark value of red.

Chroma refers to the strength of the color. Rose is a red of weakened chroma, that is, it is faded and has lessened strength or intensity.

Neutral or achromatic colors: Black, white, grays and tans having no discernible hues.

Primary colors: Bright red, lemon yellow and intense sky blue, as you will remember from kindergarten. All other colors can be mixed from them.

Secondary colors: Violet or purple (produced from a mixture of equal amounts of red and blue), orange (from red and yellow) green (from yellow and blue).

Tertiary colors: The remaining colors on the wheel, made by mixing secondary colors.

HARMONIES FROM COLOR WHEELS

If you would like to understand color theories, why not embroider your own color wheel on canvas? Divide a circle into twelve equal segments, then stitch in the colors shown, with threads of different values. Use the full hue in the middle of the segment, light values towards the top, and dark values (approaching black) towards the central point in the circle.

The color wheels which follow are from "An Easy Guide to Color for Flower Arrangers" by Margaret Dodson (published by Hearthside Press, New York). This inexpensive little guide is excellent and I do recommend it.

Complementary Color Schemes, Fig. 69.

Color complements are satisfying in a color scheme; used side by side their colors enrich each other. To avoid clashing colors, use only one primary in full chroma; use the other two in grayed tones and in the larger areas. Variations of direct complementary color schemes are split complements, Fig. 70, triads, Fig. 71, and tetrads, Fig. 72. Figs. 69, 70, 71, 72 shows their uses in color schemes.

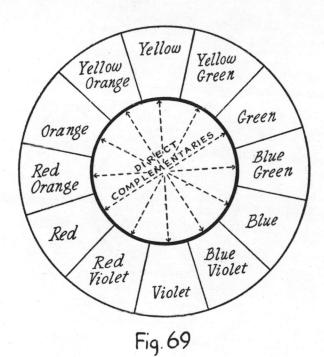

Fig. 69

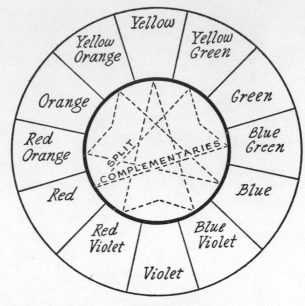

Fig. 70

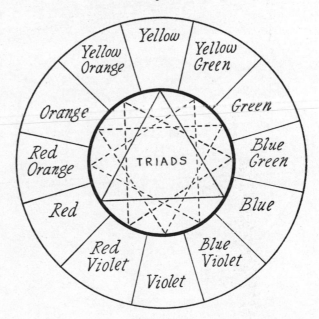

Fig. 71

See page 122 for description.

I

III

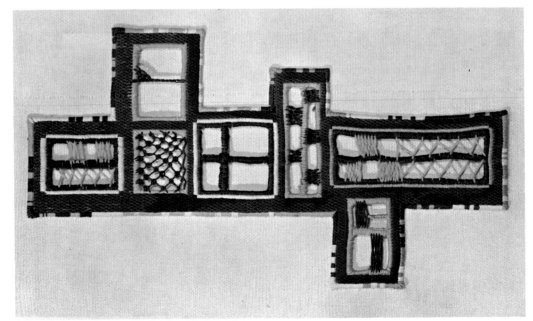

II

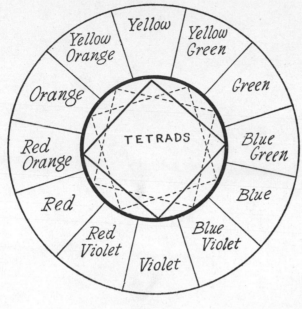

Fig. 72

Monochromatic Color Schemes

These are color schemes based on using different values of hue. Such color schemes can be very striking but also might become tiresome, therefore add contrast by using threads of different textures and light reflectance, as well as stitches that are strong opposites, such as tent stitch and rice stitch, or Gobelin droit and Smyrna cross. These are sophisticated, hard-to-do schemes. Neutral colors may be used to define areas or create shadows in monochromatic embroideries.

Analogous Color Schemes, Fig. 73.

This harmony is based on using neighboring hues related to one primary color. For instance orange, red-orange, and yellow-orange, or blue-green, blue-violet and blue. Combine light and dark values, because if neighboring hues of the same value are used, they deaden each other.

Analogous schemes create a strong sense of season. Spring, for instance, can be portrayed with pale yellows,

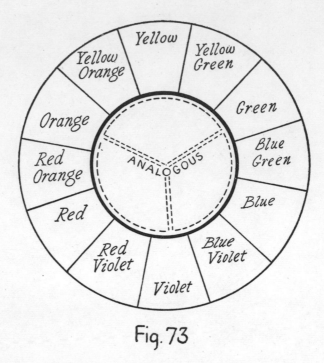

Fig. 73

pale greens, and deeper greens, for these are the colors found in Nature during that time. Blues and violets create a cool, remote, aquatic-like mood.

COLORS CREATE MOOD

Full-strength primary color combinations are in style, but color sophisticates feel that such schemes are too obvious, too clashing. If you do favor brilliant colors, however, think of the public parks in summer, their gardens vibrant with every hue and strength, yet all blending together because of the large surrounding areas of green grass and trees, as well as blue sky, to act as a tone control.

Colors have very definite effects. Blue, green and violet are cool, remote or receding colors; red, yellow and orange are hot or advancing colors. Walk through any art museum and observe the use of colors in creating a sense of nearness or of distance. The further an object in Nature, the less chromatic it becomes. Therefore, a distant roof top is painted with less intense color than one which is nearby. A mountain seen from far away is shown a grayed violet (since atmosphere adds a haziness to all objects).

POINTERS FOR WORKING OUT COLOR SCHEMES

1. Key your needlework to other colors in the room or in your costume. Use the most vivid color for your accent color; balance it with larger areas of less-intense color. Distribute the accent color in small amounts through the design for the sake of rhythm.

2. Stitches with texture will look darker than flat stitches, even when the identical color thread is used.

3. Remember that colors react differently when side by side. Complements (bright red and green, or blue and yellow) brighten each other, but they deaden grays and browns. White next to a dark color, and black next to a light color, will brighten each other.

4. When selecting a gray (or other neutral) thread to use with a clear color—for example, red—pick a gray with an undertone of red; otherwise, the gray will seem to be mixed with green.

5. The heavier the texture, the bolder and more masculine the design will seem.

PUTTING THE DESIGN ON CANVAS

There are three methods of design for canvas work, sometimes used separately, sometimes combined. An advanced canvas work embroideress will often use all three to obtain the results she wants.

The Graph Paper Method requires paper ruled into squares. Using this paper to represent squares on the canvas, color the squares to duplicate the stitch count and design of your choice (see Fig. 74). The ability to draw realistically is not necessary, since the paper is squared-off and even a child can produce designs by counting the boxes and filling them in as needed. These designs can then be reproduced exactly, with the needle, using the chart as a count guide and being careful to follow the identical count on the canvas. It is always wise to indicate the stitch you plan to use on the graph paper, since it may cover more than one square. This method is especially useful for simple repeat designs and almost essential for lettering and numerals. Figs. 74-84 shows designs suited to this method.

A less direct approach to the graph method is to place carbon paper directly under a design and graph paper under the carbon, so that you have three sheets in the following order: design, carbon, and lined paper. This method is less creative, because it usually involves a design already executed, and presents certain hazards which must be worked out. If the design is too large for the graph paper you are using, only a few squares will be filled, and the stitches will be too scattered. If the design is too small, the easiest method for enlarging it accurately is to have it photostatically enlarged to the needed size. Be sure to ask the photo enlarger for the positive image, since the negative will be white on black and difficult to see.

The Folded Paper Method of designing for oneself concerns the various ways of cutting folded paper and assembling the cuts into a design. The following procedure is helpful.

1) Using any size paper, fold exactly in half and cut out a shape: hearts, diamonds, leaves, flowers, fruits, geometrics, etc. (Fig. 85).

2) Fold the paper in half and half again. Now you can cut more complicated shapes such as stars, scallops, circles, ovals, scrolls, etc.

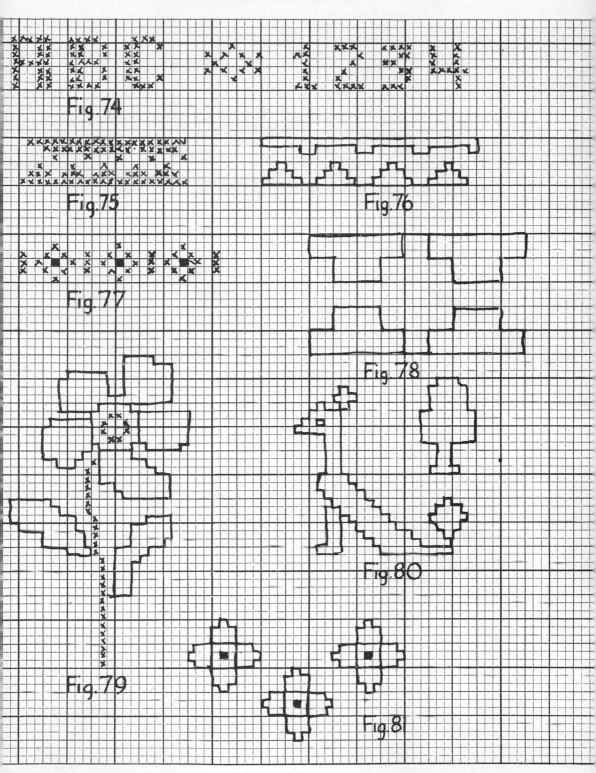

Fig. 74

Fig. 75

Fig. 76

Fig. 77

Fig. 78

Fig. 79

Fig. 80

Fig. 81

Fig. 82

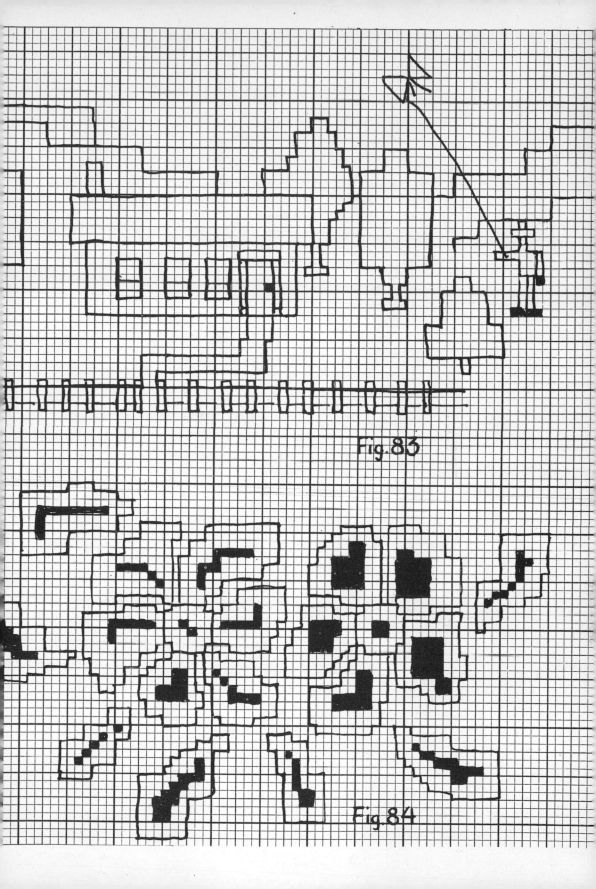

Fig. 83

Fig. 84

3) Try folding the paper in equal sections, as you would for cutting paper dolls, and you can create repeat designs of triangles, stars, flowers, leaves, scrolls, etc.

4) Assemble your cut paper shapes in a composition, keeping in mind balance and proportion in relation to the over-all size of your design.

Experiment with folded paper using different cuts and you will find many interesting shapes. Once the design has

Fig. 85

been decided on, place the cut paper patterns carefully on the canvas, properly centered and arranged. (They may be pinned or fastened with masking tape which can be removed later.) A deep blue watercolor can be used to paint carefully around the paper cut to produce an outline on the canvas. It is best to use a fine brush so that the line is distinct, but not heavy. India ink may be substituted for watercolor, if desired, but it may smudge light colored yarns, especially white. It is advisable to use crayons or colored pencil, retracing the design on paper, in order to get an idea of the colors you wish to use. This is especially desirable in helping you to visualize the design in its actual setting. If you are making a chair seat, for example, the paper cuts colored with crayons may be laid directly on the chair.

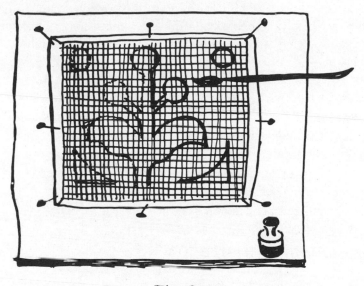

Fig. 86

The Direct Sketching Method is good for those who have some ability in drawing. In this direct approach the subject is sketched out on paper, to the exact size of the desired finished composition. Be careful to fit the design to the shape, keeping good balance and proportion. When the design has been carefully laid out in pencil, color it with crayons or pencils to show the color threads to be used. Then ink all lines with black so that they will show through the canvas. Place the canvas over the inked drawing and again with a fine brush and deep-toned water-color, paint the design on the canvas. (See Fig. 86.) Most professional embroidery designers use this method, the difference being that they paint the entire design on the canvas in oil, using a solution of one part each of linseed oil, white varnish and turpentine.

In this last method of tracing the design directly on the canvas with brush and water color, inexpensive "helps" may be purchased in shops, if one does not mind using another's work. Coloring books—some of the best are published by museums—have realistic drawings in black and white, which can be traced either entirely or in parts. Many patterns are given in this book. Ink transfers sold in needlework shops are also useful and can be traced directly, making it possible to use the same transfer many times. Many needlework shops sell booklets in which the designs have already been counted out on squared paper and colored. These are useful in obtaining ideas and for lettering styles. However, it is always most gratifying to produce one's own work.

DESIGNING WITH STITCHES

Any piece of embroidery requires constant reappraisal from inception to completion. It is often the extra stitch or addition of another color for accent that makes the finished product an individual creation. Even a prepared piece designed by a professional comes out differently when it is actually "worked" because it bears the stamp of the worker as well as that of the designer.

10. LEAVES—Wall hanging in wool and silk. Stitches: button-hole, couched buttonhole, Hungarian, Parisian, mosaic, tent, Moorish, fishbone raised, Gobelin, Roumanian couching, rice, Vandyke, Florentine, etc. Designed and worked by Author.

In designing with stitches the needlewoman can create numerous diaper patterns using any number of stitches (see Chapter III). These can be used for all-over repeat patterns or as backgrounds, and will work up nicely into rugs, bags, upholstery, and cushions. Certain stitches will produce special effects, and it is wise to consider these effects in designing. (Refer to Chapter III.)

DESIGNING WITH NATURAL FORMS

When producing designs based on natural or realistic form, keep in mind their natural color, and select stitches which can be easily shaded to produce a realistic effect. Use textured stitches to establish center of interest emphasis or accent, such as Smyrna cross to indicate a patterned fabric, or plaited stitch for a basket. Select graded silks or wools with at least four to six values of each color.

IMPRESSIONISTIC DESIGN

Interpretation of form is one of the basic ideas in embroidery and therefore impressionistic work is very adapt-

11. RUG—All wool. Stitches: Turkey knot, Gobelin, back. Designed and worked by Author.

able. A bird does not have to have each feather in place to give the impression of a bird; neither must a flower have every petal represented. Color too can be used as it suits the setting and style of the piece, and not as a pre-conceived idea that all grass is green, or all water blue. Light plays an important game with color, by causing it to change and reflect with different situations and materials.

The increasing trend in modern art toward abstractionism must be reflected in embroidery. Actually, canvas work is very well suited to the abstract approach—the paintings of Picasso or Joseph Albers could be easily interpreted in this medium. Many of the geometric abstracts are ideally suited to canvas, because of the squares in the medium. It is therefore possible to have abstract paintings on your wall, and integrated abstractions on furniture upholstery or on rugs. The action school of painting provides an interesting idea when applied to embroidery; a method of creating with color and stitch as the urge moves you. This emotional approach to color and design becomes a completely personal impression when applied to embroidery. Children are especially intrigued with it because they have no color inhibitions. Once a youngster has mastered Gobelin droit or encroaching stitch, it becomes a fascinating game for him to produce colored rugs like contemporary tapestries or Victorian rag rugs.

ADAPTING DESIGNS FOR USE

It is always important in embroidery to keep in mind the function and use of each piece, so that the stitches and color selected will be suited to the setting. Shell stitch, for example, would not work well for upholstery or rugs since it might catch on clothes or heels. To design for use is to be aware of setting, function, and color harmony.

CONSIDER THE SHAPES

Most designs can be adapted to different shapes and sizes. For example, a fish is normally an oblong shape, and would work out well on a narrow rectangular pillow. However, for

12. FOUR SEASONS—Mirror frame. Stitches include: tent, Gobelin, Florentine, Hungarian, cross, back. Designed and worked by Alice Morgan Carson.

a square stool you would squeeze the fish up and wind up with an angel fish, better suiting the shape.

Many people like integrated appointments in the home. A design taken from a rug pattern—perhaps the center medallion—could be used for sofa cushions or stool upholstery. When designing for specific purposes, keep in mind the **idea** of representation, do not clutter the piece. In designing a fire screen around the theme of family hobbies, do not get carried away and attempt to depict all hobbies. It is better to sort out the subject matter in general catagories such as sports, crafts, and games, and try to depict a few of these in general terms.

ECCLESIASTICAL AND HERALDIC EMBROIDERY

"Had I the heavens' embroidered cloths,
Enwrought with gold and silver leaf"

Yeats' poetic wish for the cloth of Heaven points up the special appropriateness of gold and silver for religious use but, in general, religious and secular color symbolism is the same. Although it is somewhat beyond the scope of this book to discuss in detail the colors suitable for ecclesiastical embroidery, the following general observations may be made: white symbolizes purity; red, martyrdom and love; green, faith and immortality; gold, divine light; violet, sacrifice and penitence; blue, spirituality; yellow, bright sun; orange, warmth.

Keep in mind, when selecting colors for church ornamentation, that blues and violets fade away under cold artificial light. These receding colors are also lost when seen in shadowed areas.

Light colors carry better than dark ones. Against a dark background, fully chromatic colors show up well; brilliant yellow or red are excellent against gray stone; orange or yellow against wood.

Ecclesiastical canvas work requires rather specific designs. Before attempting it, consult the minister, priest or rabbi and, if possible, the church architect. Many simple patterns which are interesting to make and will enrich the

13. KNEELER—Stitches: Hungarian, straight cross, cross, tent, herringbone couching, Gobelin; wool and gold thread. Designed and worked by Author.

14. PULPIT FALL—Stitches: tent, buttonhole, Hungarian, bokhara couching, stem, straight cross, herringbone couching, fringe in long Turkey knot. Wool. Designed and worked by Author.

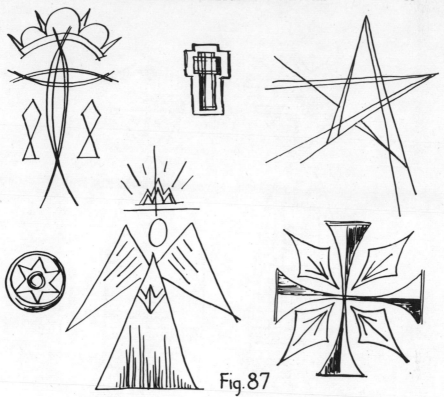

Fig. 87

church for many years can be devised for pew kneelers. A few possibilities are shown in Fig. 87. The design should suit the setting of the church, be it Gothic or contemporary, and the colors should harmonize with the other furnishings.

Many women's groups have turned out needlemade rugs as a joint project, each working separate sections which are eventually joined to form the whole. Such a rug was executed by a group of twenty women from Pittsburgh, for the steps of the Altar in the National Cathedral in Washington, D.C. In fact, the National Cathedral has become richly endowed with many excellent pieces of canvas work produced by women from all over the United States.

Canvas embroidery has always adapted well to heraldry and coats-of-arms. And while the blazoning of family insignia is rare in America, the custom persists here in the seals and insignia of colleges and cities. Several excellent

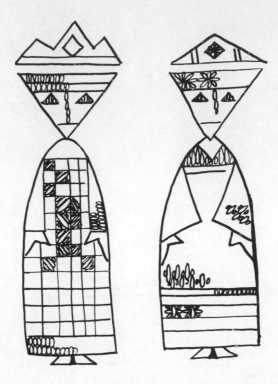

books on heraldic as well as ecclesiastical design are available and should be consulted by an embroiderer who wishes to work in these fields.

COLOR AND DESIGN IN PERIOD DECORATION

The surest method for designing embroidery to fit a period room is to take your motif from an accessory which is in the mood you wish; an oriental rug, a primitive painting, a Williamsburg fabric, a Japanese screen, a Chinese porcelain—from any of these you can abstract a border or a theme for your needle. The names of the stitches can be surprisingly useful in helping you select the appropriate stitch. Here are some additional design motifs listed according to furniture styles.

15. SPANISH SAMPLER—Wool and silk, predominantly red and white. Stitches: tent, Hungarian, Florentine, rice, cross, flat. Designed and worked by Author.

American

Early American: Tent stitch used a great deal during Colonial times. Turkey work for upholstery. Checkerboard and zig-zags. Scallops. Rough tweedy yarns, simple colors. Motifs: Roosters, simple flower motifs.

Pennsylvania Dutch: Hex signs, hearts, tulips, used in threes to symbolize trinity; four-leaf clover.

Spanish and Mexican: Lots of white spiked with pungent brilliant colors. Scrolls to simulate wrought iron. Cactus and other tropical foliage.

American Georgian: Acanthus leaf, scrolls, shells, leaves, husks, gadrooning, chinoiserie, India print motifs. Simulated velvet. Turkey work still popular. Florentine stitches in some upholstery.

Federal Empire: Motifs from Oriental rugs, Currier and Ives prints. Silk threads. Blues, greens, grays. Acanthus leaf, laurel leaf, lyre, lion's mask. Gobelin stitch, and long-armed cross-stitch also used.

English

Chippendale: Rich colorful fabrics. Design from Chinese porcelain and other Chinese motifs particularly suitable. Many floral sprays; also eagle head, bamboo. Chinese red. Close-stitch embroidery.

Hepplewhite: Garlands, three ostrich plumes, wheat, ovals, serpentine curves, narrow stripes. Soft greens, blues, pink. Silks and satins.

Adam: All classical motifs delicately reproduced. Honeysuckle, urns, floral swags, roses, pineapple, fuchsia, acanthus leaves, rams head, griffin, many birds. Colors: Green, light grays and blues, pale mauve, some coral. See Wedgwood designs of this period.

Sheraton: Plain stripes; pastel blue predominant with white, black or yellow.

Georgian: Designs based on India prints, gold tapestry; look of elegance.

Later Georgian styles: Acanthus leaf, classical motifs. Floral wreaths, swags, lyre, graceful urn.

Victorian: Large fruits, flowers, nosegays, leaves, roses, beading. Horsehair and plush fabrics. Bright red, dark green and gold. Turkey tufting popular for birds and animals; cross-stitch used generally. From approximately 1850 to 1915, chart designs for Berlin wool work popular in America.

French

Regency: Sunburst, cornucopia, honeysuckle, acanthus leaf. Gold and vibrant colors against dark tones. Much needlepoint. Gobelins and Aubussons popular for wall hangings.

Provincial: Motifs from toile de Jouy prints, checked ginghams. Faded blues and reds. Many different kinds of embroidery popular.

Empire: Spears, stars with laurel leaf, mythological birds and animals, swans, lion's feet, lyres, octagons. Savonnerie weaves. Vibrant deep colors. Black with gold and silver ornamentation.

PROCEDURE FOR CANVAS EMBROIDERY

1. Decide on the article you wish to embroider; consider its purpose, size, color, use. If you are a beginner, don't be over-ambitious.

2. Pick your design. (See earlier sections in this chapter.)

3. Put your design on canvas. (See Putting the Design on Canvas, Chapter IV.)

4. Select the stitches from Chapter III. Make a record of the stitches you selected on a simple paper pattern.

5. Bind off the edges of the canvas.

6. Stitch the most complicated and shaded areas first, the background last.

7. See Chapter V for the necessary finishing details.

Blocking and Mounting

The finishing touches—washing, blocking and mounting—are easy compared to the painstaking work of embroidering the canvas, but they get a disproportionate share of attention if neglected. A careless stitch is quickly overlooked, but a soiled canvas or poor blocking job cannot be missed.

WASHING

Even the most careful worker will get some smudges on her work. "Woolite" or mild liquid soaps are the best washing solutions. (Before washing, trace the shape on muslin to make blocking easier.) Dip the piece into the washing solution several times, but do not wring or squeeze it. Thoroughly rinse in warm, never hot, water. Lay flat on several clean dry towels and carefully roll to soak up the excess water. Unroll and block.

BLOCKING

Since very little canvas work is still mounted in a frame in this country, you must learn the proper blocking technique. Lay the washed piece, face up, on a clean wooden board which has been covered with soft muslin. Carefully shape the piece to its original dimensions and secure all around with tacks. Since wool and silk will shrink very slightly, be sure to keep the tacks about one inch apart. Always nail tacks to excess skrim and never put nails through the actual work. (See Fig. 88.) Most Penelope and single mesh canvas have been pre-stiffened with a starch

Fig.88

and what remains after washing will keep your piece from puffing up.

MOUNTING

Most upholstery work should be mounted by a professional upholstery firm. This includes bags and pocketbooks, which must have linings and handles. Cushions and pillows may be mounted at home, if you are handy with a sewing machine. Small rugs, no more than approximately two by three feet, may also be mounted at home. Burlap makes good rug backing and fringe can be made by using extra long turkey knot on the edges. Pictures, wall hangings, sweater decorations, coasters, and suspenders can also be mounted in the home with the aid of linings and a sewing machine.

Rug Mounting In mounting rugs that are to have two sides fringed, turn back the canvas, allowing only one row to show; work long turkey knot along this edge. Fold back the other two sides. Work Gobelin or buttonhole stitch through both thicknesses. Then hem the lining to the back, covering all four canvas edges, Fig. 89.

If fringe is not desired, buttonhole may be worked, turning back the canvas and working through two thicknesses all the way around.

Picture Mounting   "Sobo" white paste glue is best for picture mounting.

Under glass: Glue the washed, blocked canvas to heavy cardboard, and do not worry about the edges of the canvas. If you basted them or if they are bound with tape, simply leave as is as the picture matting will cover this part.

Without glass: you may also mount hangings on plywood, masonite, buckram, and wood-backed foam-rubber. Tufted or three-dimensional embroidery should be mounted in a recessed frame, similar to découpage work.

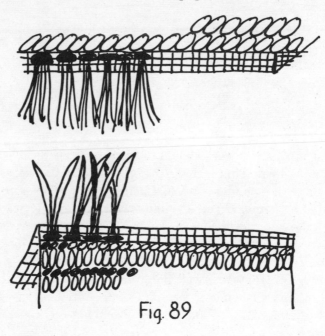

Fig. 89

Mounting Cushions Soft material-backed cushions are fairly easy to mount, and require only sewing, material, welting and stuffing. Stuffing may be either cotton, goose down, foam rubber, or modern substitutes for these materials. It is your preference. Hand sewing is not always suc-

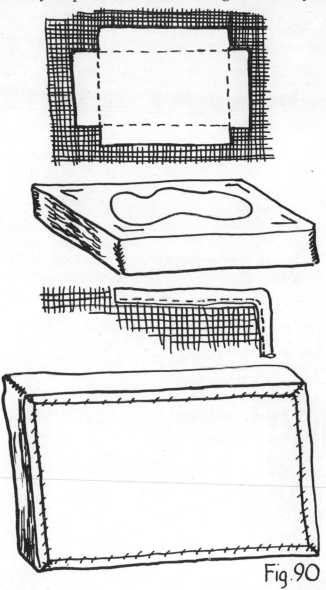

Fig. 90

cessful and most soft cushions are best done with machine stitching. Suitable backing materials are velvet, heavy cotton, linen, wool, burlap and nylon or dacron combinations.

However, square cushions with canvas sides can be made up also, either for seats or as chuch kneelers, Fig. 90. With these cushions, the top and four sides are worked in one piece. Foam rubber makes an excellent, firm stuffing and can be cut to the exact size. Sew the four side seams of canvas together with matching wool, insert the cushion, and hem felt or heavy linen to the bottom. You may also use rubberized hair, cotton batting or any suitable pillow stuffing.

JOINING CANVAS

When it is impossible to make up the entire design (rugs particularly) on one piece of canvas, two or more matching canvases are used. These pieces are joined together in the following manner:

The two sides of canvas are laid together, matching all holes. Then the design or border is worked over the two thicknesses. Tent stitch, Gobelin, cross, or straight cross are excellent for this joining operation. (See Fig. 91.)

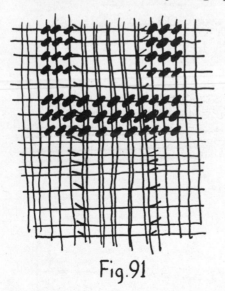

Fig. 91

Procedures for Teachers and Suppliers

In an age and country where virtually all processes in textiles are limited by what the machines can mass produce, appreciation of original, hand-crafted merchandise has never been higher. Unfortunately, in America the craft of embroidery, unlike weaving, pottery, wood carving, or ceramics, has fallen far behind that of Europe for several reasons. Ours is a fast-moving civilization and embroidery is a slow process. Also the necessary time for apprenticeship is not always available. Consequently, for the past two generations little information about techniques has been passed along from older embroiderers. As a result, there are few teachers in America today who are qualified to give both technical and creative instruction in embroidery. Another reason why American embroidery lags behind Europe is that—although there are books dealing with all fields of the craft—far too many prefer to be jack-of-all-trades, rather than master of one or two. This dilettante approach may be easy and pleasant, but it does not produce dedicated needlewomen.

In the years preceding the turn of the century, embroidery was taught in America as a truly creative endeavor. As a result, original and beautiful work was a rule, rather than an exception. Of course, we cannot nor do we wish to turn the clock back, but those of us who love embroidery have high hopes that the coming years will see a renaissance in the field. We forecast that the interest in needlework—now

16. NO 9—Part of an abstract series on the golden rectangle. Stitches: Gobelin, encroaching Gobelin, Turkey knot, rice, Parisian, Hungarian, Florentine, cutwork, spider filling, cretan filling, fern. In wool, silk and cotton applied to velvet ground. Designed and worked by Author.

fairly wide but comparatively shallow—will be deepened and strengthened as more and more people discover the joy, satisfaction and sense of creativity which fine embroidery can bring.

RECOMMENDED REQUIREMENTS FOR TEACHERS

To supplement the small group of American teachers, we are fortunate in having a number of well-qualified British teachers, many of them graduated from the Royal School of Needlework in London or from the British art colleges where embroidery is included in the curriculum. Although embroidery is in the textile field, it deals primarily with shape interpretation, color, and technique. Therefore, most principles of design apply to it.

In order to raise the standards, I recommend that teachers qualify themselves in many if not all of the following ways. My recommendations are based on the examinations offered by the London City Guilds, in England.

(1) Art major in college, or some formal training at a design or art school. No matter how talented, no one can teach others unless she understands design principles, including color.

(2) Special study of historical embroidery, including close attention to museum collections. As an example, no one can teach underside couching, the method used for gold work in the thirteenth century, without having studied its background and function.

(3) Membership in recognized craft guilds to foster and promote creative work. Most states have craftsman guilds, with a jury of admission required to pass on the qualifications of prospective members. The standards are high, and any one who gains admission has the satisfaction of working for the highest goals in the craft.

(4) Special classes with certified and established embroidery teachers, or at schools where particular fields of embroidery are taught.

(5) A knowledge of textiles from actual work in the field, including materials, equipment, and tools necessary to the craft.

(6) Examinations in all fields of embroidery in which one anticipates teaching. These examinations are offered annually by the American branch of the Embroiderer's Guild, in New York.

(7) Competitive exhibitions to encourage a high standard of design and technique. Exhibitions whet the imagination and awaken a keener interest for visitors as well as participants. (Chapter VII on exhibitions has further suggestions.)

(8) Study educational methods which teach how to encourage, instruct and stimulate creativity in students.

17. & 18. TWO FLORENTINE PIL-
LOWS—Colors: reds, golds, yellows, oranges, some blue; in wool. Designed and
worked by Author.

See page 122 for description.

IV

V

THE CLASSROOM

After a teacher has established her qualifications, a place to teach must be considered. Classes in different kinds of embroidery are offered in craft schools and public schools, in churches, museums, and civic buildings. Art groups, Y's, adult education departments, and even needlework shops (if they have space), are logical sponsors for needlework classes.

In my opinion, the approach to embroidery in public schools needs revision. Many public schools do offer training in technique as part of home economics, but there is little guidance in the aesthetics of embroidery (which could be a function of the art department). Yet, of all the art crafts, embroidery has the widest application: in the apparel field, in home decoration, in the church and, as anyone will agree who has seen the magnificent hangings on the "S.S. France," in fine art.

Mention should be made of the fact that there are several craft schools in the East which offer intensive training in stitchery, crewel and canvas work, and the trend is spreading to Florida, California and Texas. Craft schools in Kentucky and Tennessee are enlarging the horizons for high quality, commercial embroidery by selling hand-quilted articles through New York's most exclusive specialty shops.

Beginning classes for adults in the various fields of embroidery usually run on an 8- to 12-week schedule, meeting once weekly for 2-hour sessions with added homework. In a beginning class in canvas work, for example, the teacher decides how many stitches will be taught and the length and duration of home assignments for practice. In an 8-week course, it is possible to cover 16 to 20 stitches, as well as aspects of color, shading, shape, interpretation, and design; this enables most students to go on to self-expression in the medium.

CLASSES FOR CHILDREN

Classes for children require special handling and patience to allow each child to be self-expressive while learning tech-

19. HOUSE—Stitches: tent, Hungarian, Florentine, mosaic, Gobelin, web, back, and long-and-short stitch for the trees. Designed by Norton Peterson. Worked by Mrs. Jack Levy (student).

nical procedure. Canvas work is particularly adaptable to the young people's ability since it can be worked to the counted thread (which they enjoy doing) and many children produce work almost equal in technique to adult efforts. The corporate project, for instance a large rug or mural worked on by the entire class, is also highly successful with children.

Since embroidery requires individual attention as well as class participation, the number of students is usually small. However, some teachers can handle large groups successfully and the size of the class, therefore, is dependent on the teacher's realistic estimate of his or her ability to handle all the students effectively.

EMBROIDERY AS THERAPY

Certain types of embroidery are ideally suited for rehabilitation treatment in hospitals and clinics. Canvas work in particular, because of the rhythm involved in the stitching and thread counting, has a soothing and relaxing effect. In addition, it does not make a great many physical demands, nor require much equipment; this makes it ideal for bed patients as well as convalescents.

Quite apart from the relaxation it offers the patients, canvas embroidery is also useful in workshop classes designed to restore disabled persons to gainful employment. It does not require much equipment and even severely handicapped patients can master the basic procedure. The salability of simple embroidered articles such as rugs, pillows, belts, bookcovers, etc. is another asset which can be credited to the account of canvas embroidery in a rehabilitation program.

It might be appropriate to mention the Craft School at Penn Alps, Pennsylvania. Here, residents of isolated, economically underprivileged communities are taught to be selfsupporting. There is need for more schools like this one.

THE EQUIPMENT

A good reference library is essential for the teacher. Books, magazines, and all the literature of the field with new

20. & 21. SCREEN—Seven panel. Stitches used include: tent, Parisian, Florentine, jacquard, long-armed cross, Gobelin, web, and mosaic. Designed by Alice Morgan Carson, worked by Mrs. H. M. M. Nicholas.

approaches should be read; they will provide many ideas. Both practical and historical literature should find a place on the reference shelf. It is helpful to keep a notebook of ideas, with an envelope for wools, silks, threads of different textures, interesting color combinations, and similar useful materials.

Specific equipment depends on the field of embroidery which is being taught. In crewel and white work, a hoop is needed by both student and teacher; it is unnecessary in canvas work.

caption opposite

For canvas embroidery, the following teaching aids are useful: **A blackboard** and chalk music-liner for diagramming count stitches and enlarging the work for all to see. Small samples of work for students to handle, and slides of both contemporary and traditional embroidery, can give the student insight into the limitless possibilities. **Crayons and watercolors** are necessary for indicating shading changes on designs, and a **small fine brush** for outlining designs on canvas. The sampler method of instruction is helpful for beginning students, because it gives practice in stitches. A color wheel made of yarn (see page 60) would be instructive and interesting; encourage each student to make his own wheel.

EMBROIDERY SHOPS

It is not at all unusual for needlework shops to offer lessons as part of their activity. Unfortunately, a great many shops also feel compelled to sell to beginners the ubiquitous kits and stamped goods and the embroidery cotton for working them. In my experience, not enough shops carry a representative range of materials needed for creative work. I am therefore listing what I consider is minimum equipment for a well-stocked store:

(1) Canvas, both Penelope, single mesh, and hemp for making rugs.

(2) At least one good grade of even-weave linen and one grade of ecclesiastical linen; burlap.

(3) Wooden hoops, embroidery needles, thimbles, scissors, embroidery frames, transfer pencils, tracing paper, masking tape.

(4) A good selection of threads—wool, crewel wool, linen, cotton, Pearsall's filoselle washable silk, filofloss silk, decorative braids and cords, jap-gold, colored strings, raffia, and synthetics.

(5) Transfers, books on design, and a wide selection of titles explaining methods on different kinds of embroidery.

Many shops exhibit examples of finished pieces, particularly of those made from kits. A fine display of original work, perhaps even a small exhibit of pieces completed by local craftsmen, would also stimulate interest. A list of local designers, teachers and professional embroideresses would benefit the shop as well as the public. Ecclesiastical embroidery is always needed and informed and capable retailers can be influential in fostering better design.

CANDIDATES FOR TEACHING ACCREDITATION

If you are a candidate for accreditation as a certified embroidery teacher, you no doubt will be required to pass an examination along the following lines. Examinations of a similar sort are given by the London City Guilds, and by several private embroidery schools in America. Earlier in this chapter, I recommended general requirements; I repeat the specific musts here:

a) Master all the stitches suited to the particular embroidery medium in which you are being tested. You should know not only the stitches themselves, but also understand their virtues as well as their limitations in creative interpretation.

b) Learn the history of the embroidery. Be sure to visit or otherwise familiarize yourself with the collections in your field.

c) Demonstrate your ability to design embroidery under examination conditions.

d) Submit examples of your work (at least 2 are required). Study the books in your field and keep abreast of the new literature as it is published.

7

Embroidery for Use and Exhibition

Canvas embroidery has many practical uses. For centuries, it has covered the person, decorated the house and adorned the church. Using any of the long-wearing stitches (tent, Gobelin, Hungarian, mosaic, chequer, Scotch, Florentine, cross, straight cross, Smyrna, rice, fern, long-legged, etc.), canvas will last a lifetime and, in many cases, longer. It would be impossible to name all the articles which can be made from embroidered canvas. A partial listing follows; other possibilities are shown in the plates.

EXHIBITIONS

In recent years, many groups have sponsored needlework exhibitions. A standard for shows is fairly well established, although local differences do exist.

1. **Rules and Regulations:** Written rules give information about place, date, opening and closing time, deadline for receiving and removing entries, entry fees (if any), insurance, and prizes. The name, address and telephone number of the person who can be consulted may be included. If there is a theme, it should be stated.

Catalogues listing each entry by number and description are frequently prepared. The catalog may also give the Rules and Regulations, the theme, scale of points, and other information which is pertinent.

Policy decisions must be made in advance by the sponsoring group. For instance, according to accepted standards, all embroidery must be hand-worked by the exhibitor; packaged designs and kits are not acceptable. Rules must cover this point.

Consideration may be given to beginners and junior groups; separate classes for their entries would encourage them to exhibit.

2. **Classification of Entries:** There are three major divisions into which the entries are grouped. Exhibitors should state on their entry card which classification is to apply. Although the articles are not necessarily displayed in this order, it provides the exhibition committee with a general idea for planning space and exhibition requirements. Ecclesiastical objects require proper staging and it is very helpful to know what materials will be needed to display them advantageously. The divisions are:

a) Household or Decorative Arts

Rugs	Picture and Picture Frames
Stair Carpeting	Wall Hangings
Upholstery	Fire Screens
Pillows and Cushions	Bell Pulls
Book Covers	Coasters
Tie Backs	Valances

b) Personal Accessories
Belts
Slippers and suspenders
Glass cases, wallets, pincushions
Cumberbunds and vests
Sweater decorations and buttons

c) Ecclesiastical
Kneelers, rugs, carpeting
Banners and book covers
Vestments and orpheys
Upholstery, book markers, pulpit falls

3. **Acceptable Techniques:** The type of embroidery work acceptable in the exhibition must be named. Occasionally, hooking and tatting will be included under acceptable techniques. Knitting and crocheting are not generally considered embroidery.

22. FIG TREE—One of a set of ten chair seats, each featuring a different fruit tree. Designed by Mona Spoor.

The major techniques always included are: Canvas Work, Crewel, Gold Work, Cut Work and White Work (including drawn and pulled thread work), Stitchery (including combinations of several techniques such as pulled work and crewel), and sometimes Hooking, Tatting, Lace Work and Macrame (making hand-tied braids and fringes).

JUDGING

Most recognized exhibitions have a Jury of Selections and Awards, whose duty it is not only to award prizes and ribbons, but also to select the entries for exhibit. However, some exhibitions have only a Jury of Award. The catalogue, the Rules and Regulations, or both, should specify which kind of jury will be provided.

Exhibitors are rated on a point scoring or percentage system. Following is a typical scale for evaluating the entries. Note that a perfect score of 100 per cent is never given, since perfection is considered an impossibility.

Craftsmanship (technique)	50%
Design (choice, originality and interpretation)	30%
Color (its harmony and placement or rhythm)	10%
Suitability (practical and usable)	5%
Appearance (neat, clean, well-mounted)	5%
	100%

Note that color, although actually an element of design, is listed separately. In effect, this gives design a total scale of 40%.

Selecting the judges. Judges are selected from three major groups: designers or artists, embroidery teachers or professionals, and museum curators. Three judges are considered an adequate jury and their decision is always final. Almost all juries are selected for their knowledge of the craft to be judged. It follows, then, that an artist who lacks knowledge of embroidery, or a museum curator whose field is anthropology, cannot evaluate needlework. Judges fees may be paid out of the entry charges, or underwritten completely by the sponsoring organization when finances are no problem.

STAGING

It is the responsibility of the Staging Committee at any show to display the exhibits so that they appear at their best. This does not mean that elaborate decorations are required—in fact they should be quite simple, so that the embroideries can dominate. I have seen some really fine work displayed with such clutter that it detracted from the beauty of the piece and I thought I was back in old Aunt Sophia's attic. Proper lighting, glass cases, arrangement of objects in composition, backdrops, pedestals and platforms, color themes, continuity, all must be considered if an exhibition is to be presented well.

First, the space allocated for the exhibit should be drawn on paper (¼ inch = 1 foot) so that the Staging Committee may plan in advance where to use settings, hanging material, and display cases, to their best advantage, while still allowing for a free flow of visiting traffic. Doors, windows, electric light, radiators, etc. all should be marked. If the room is very large, free-standing center panels should be used to break up the center area and allow for additional hanging and grouping space. An easy-to-assemble back drop or room divider may be constructed out of stripping lumber and covered on both sides with heavy cardboard stapled to the wood and painted an appropriate color. Unless the exhibit is heavily insured, attractive glass cases, hanging or free standing, should be used for all small items such as eyeglass cases, wallets, slippers, etc.

Second, an artistic and attractive display of grouped items will require proper lighting. Once the show has been laid out, consideration should be given to spotlights and focalpoint lighting, particularly if the show is held in quarters with insufficient daylight or if the show is open during evening hours. Lighting should complement the color scheme. Sometimes filters of different hues (reds, blues, etc.) are used to soften white light or to effect a unity of blend in the same way a watercolor painting may have a wash tone used over the entire picture. If there is one printed sign, lettered neatly, the theme should state the exhibit. It should be well positioned and lighted. Signs should also be placed to name and describe any classes.

Third, additional equipment not usually available in galleries, museums, or art centers may be needed. If you are using colored cloth as back drops, or borrowing special lighting effects, a complete list of these needs should be compiled well in advance, insured, and arrangements made for their prompt return.

23. VIOLETS AND LEAVES—A handbag worked entirely in tent stitch; designed by Janet Shook.

24. FAUNA—A handbag featuring tent stitch; designed by Mona Spoor.

Fourth, a good working committee and the times and dates for their meetings must be established. Among the duties to be assigned are: General Chairman, Staging (including return of borrowed equipment and dismantling entries), Classification, Judging, Publicity, Ticket, and perhaps Printing. If a handy man is necessary his duties should be plainly outlined. Careful advance planning is necessary—especially when a printed, numbered catalogue must be prepared—to insure that the correct number of each entry is printed.

THEMES

Both visitors and exhibitors seem to enjoy the exhibition planned around a theme. The whole show, including the staging, the publicity, etc. should adhere to the stated theme. Here are some possible themes, which could be further developed.

Fruit and Floral Festival. This theme could include all naturalistic and abstract forms in which fruit or floral designs are depicted. It could be divided into two sections.

1) Flowers and Fruits from around the world; Oriental Gardens. The French Fleur-de-Lis. Tropical flowers and fruits. Ocean plants. Holland Tulips. Vegetables.

(2) Four Seasons of Fruits and Flowers; chrysanthemums and apples for fall. Lilies-of-the-valley and roses for spring. Poinsettias and oranges for winter. Lilies and strawberries for summer.

History and the Needle. This theme offers possibilities for using both antique and contemporary work.

1) History from many lands; work depicting Dutch scenes, Biblical subjects, historical maps, samplers from specific countries, specific historical events.

2) Contemporary to our times; map samplers, invited work from other states and countries, centennial work.

3) A display of antique embroidery equipment including, bone needles, old frames, work baskets, etc.

Religious Fashions Through the Ages. Antique and contemporary pieces exhibited together with photographs showing their actual placement in their permanent home. The show could be divided into Christian, Jewish and other, possibly borrowing antique Indian or African work.

1) Christian—vestments, church furnishings

2) Hebrew—vestments, synagogue appointments

3) Other—Medicine man headdress, Indian ceremonial pieces, chief priest vestments, Buddhist Monk robes, etc.

25. BIBLE FRUITS AND FLOWERS—One of ten altar kneelers, this shows single mesh painted canvas ready to be worked. Designed and painted by Georgiana Brown Harbeson.

Birds and Animals from Everywhere. A theme like this could include abstract and naturalistic contemporary subject matter, both fact and fantasy.

1) Biblical animals and birds; the ox, dove, lion, bull, etc.

2) Imaginary animals and birds; the unicorn, the blue ox, calico cat, fairy-tale animals.

3) Birds and animals from nature; circus animals, desert animals, sea animals, etc.

4) A booth of small hand-embroidered items for sale; toy animals, bird handbags, etc.

Cones, Spheres, and Cylinders. A completely contemporary show using moods as sub-titles, such as, Imaginative, Sophisticated, Carefree, Melancholy, Tranquil, Happy, etc.

AWARDS AND REWARDS

In the large inclusive craft exhibitions cash prizes are usually awarded. This stimulates and encourages the best craftsmen to exhibit. Incidentally, the cash prize also helps to defray the exhibitor's expenses for packing, postage and entry. The prizes are usually offered by suppliers of materials and sponsoring groups or patrons. They should be solicited well in advance of the exhibition.

Ribbons are also awarded as prizes when no cash prizes are offered. In embroidery exhibitions a first (blue), second and third are offered in the three major classifications and sometimes a design award, making a total of not more than ten ribbons; occasionally an honorable mention also will be offered. Rather than force the judges to select winners from each class whether or not they are worthy, I think that judges should be allowed to withhold ribbons in divisions which have insufficient or inadequate entries, to do otherwise degrades the exhibition and lowers the standard for the craft.

The prize system, whether ribbons or cash awards, may not be the ultimate success you think it should be, but it is the established method in most crafts.

SELLING ENTRIES

Although many exhibitions do not permit sale of entries, there are just as many that do. It is a question of decision by the sponsoring groups. Exhibitions serve a worthwhile purpose in presenting the public with a summary of contemporary and traditional work. A public that has an opportunity to see and think is a public that appreciates and selects.

HOW TO BE A GOOD EXHIBITOR

The good exhibitor is, first of all a good sport. Everyone likes the public recognition which comes from exhibiting and later, perhaps, from winning, but far more important is the realization that winner as well as loser both have profited from the Show.

Not infrequently, a would-be exhibitor has his entry rejected. Juries do not always agree, and it is quite possible that a reject in one show will win a prize in another. However, if a piece of work has been rejected for inclusion in several shows, it should be apparent that the work is not up to accepted standards. Therefore, the worker had better apply his persistence to starting another canvas.

Other craft exhibitions: Aside from exhibitions devoted to embroidery, there are local or national craft exhibitions which accept embroidery along with weaving, pottery, jewelry, and metal work. The amateur embroideress should realize that competition in such exhibitions can be quite stiff; there are more competitors, for one, and the other craftsman may have established reputations, thereby reducing the prospects for winning. Of course, this should not deter any exhibitor from trying.

CLASSIFYING THE EXHIBITORS

To improve the general standard of exhibitions, and to enable needleworkers to compete with others who are more or less at their level of ability and experience, an order of classification is essential. Craft organizations and leading embroidery experts throughout the country have contributed, directly or indirectly, to the following recommendations:

Amateur: Engages in needlework as an avocation; he may not own or be gainfully employed by an individual or company listed in the Commercial or Professional classifications.

Commercial: Covers those who sell services or materials directly related to the embroidery craft, including those who employ Professionals and Technicians. Here are some examples:

An embroidery technician is gainfully employed for embroidery stitching, mounting, blocking, repairing and restoring embroidery, etc., **but not designing.**

Any business selling services such as mounting, blocking, repair and restoration of needlework, or producing machine or hand-embroidered articles for sale.

Any business selling yarns, threads, designs and other materials necessary to the craft, or offering qualified instruction.

Professional: This group is divided into two classifications; Teachers and Professional Embroiderers.

A teacher is qualified and certified, whenever possible, to teach one or more types of embroidery.

A professional embroiderer is a designer-craftsman, certified, recognized and qualified to teach and design, and actively engaged in producing embroidery of high standard in both design and technique.

To design effectively for embroidery one must have a wide knowledge of stitches and their uses. Therefore the artist who designs embroidery but does not know technique, and the skilled technician who can execute any stitch but is unable to design, may not be classed as a professional.

The Contemporary Approach to Embroidery

Each century, each decade, each country, has added its imprint to embroidery; this is what keeps the craft a living and dynamic one. The British Isles, Norway, Sweden, Denmark and France have made important contributions, but the role of the United States should not be minimized. From American Indians came porcupine-quill work; from pioneer women, extensive knowledge of plant dyes; from contemporary American scientists, synthetic yarns and fabrics.

In view of this heritage, and our general interest in the arts and crafts, as well as the lively competitive spirit for which America is famous, it seems strange that we should be content with a tenth-rate position in the world of embroidery. One has only to visit the "hobby shows" and so-called "art-needlework" exhibits—poorly staged and displayed, dominated by "do-it-yourself" kits rather than real craftsmanship—to realize that our standards are very low indeed.

What can be done to raise them? **First,** it seems to me that all who are interested in needlework—professionals, amateurs, commercial groups—must aim to restore "aesthetic quality." **Second,** we must educate the public, or at least that segment of it which appreciates the arts and crafts, through better craft exhibitions. The exhibitions presented by the Museum of Contemporary Crafts in New York may serve as a guide, as they are always effectively staged, well-organized, and usually offer the highest standard of work.

Third, we must conduct educational campaigns to reach craft teachers, schools, architects, interior-designers—putting them on notice that American embroidery is no longer provincial, stagnant, rampantly commercial, but ready to take its place in a dynamic modern world. Canvas work designs for chair upholstery by Picasso, and some twenty hangings by Pablo Buchard and Joseph Cantienti (executed by Mildred T. Johnstone of Bethlehem, Pennsylvania) are examples of the possibilities this medium offers. **Fourth,** there must be a synthesis of approach between embroiderers and other designers, architects, technicians and artists. Our homes, schools, offices, and churches are built to suit present-day needs, not the needs of our ancestors; embroidery too should reflect this contemporary quality. Certainly there was this synthesis in the past. Consider the eleventh century Bayeux Tapestry, designed by an artist for the Cathedral at Bayeux, France, and embroidered, not woven, in wool. It is of the highest artistic and historical importance, depicting the story of King Harold and the Norman Conquest. All too often we forget that its story was contemporaneous with its time and a synthesis between artist, embroideress, architect, and technician, as necessary today as it was then. In our day, we have the example of the Church Architectural Guild of America who have combined the talents of the clergy, architect, artist and layman—"fine arts in the service of the church."

Modern artists in other media have met the challenge of the times. Whether or not you like the results, you must admit that twentieth-century painting and sculpture are imaginative and stimulating, full of originality and artistic activity. Potters, weavers, silversmiths, architects, and artisans all have discarded the restrictive concepts of earlier traditions, and are using materials with increased sensitivity for their inherent quality and functions. This is not to say that the ancient traditions have been abandoned, but simply that they have been applied to our own age with sincerity and honesty, not with self-imposed handicaps. It is well to remember that had the embroiderers of one century copied only from earlier ones, most of our heritage would have been lost; so in a real sense, we have an obligation to tomorrow to produce work born of our **own** creative impulse.

There are some hopeful signs of a revolution in American embroidery scenes. The late Mariska Karasz, and more recently David Von Dommelen and Evi Peri, have had great impact on our field. Georgiana Brown Harbeson—continuing to interpret age-old techniques with imagination and spirit —and many other professionals whose work is less well known, are making important contributions. Victor D'Amico, Director of Education, Museum of Modern Art, New York, discussing arts and craftsmanship in "Craft Horizons" writes, "The true craftsman places his individuality above all else, and his work bears his identity." American embroidery will reach mature stature only when this is fully understood.

I once read an old Chinese proverb, originally meant for the painter, which I have altered as follows:

Embroidery is the surface applied to a textile with the hairs of an animal, the spinnings of a worm, the growings of a plant, and the efforts of a scientist, through the eye of a needle.

BIBLIOGRAPHY

Encyclopedia of Needlework. Hearthside Press, Inc. New York (Should be in every library)

American Needlework, by Georgiana Brown Harbeson. Crown Publishers, Inc. New York

Canvas Embroidery, by Hebe Cox. Mills & Boon Ltd. London

Embroidery Design and Stitches, by Kathleen Mann. Morrison & Gibb Ltd. London

English Historical Embroidery, by Barbara Snook. B. T. Batsford Ltd. London

Canvas Work & Design, by Jennifer Gray. B. T. Batsford Ltd. London

English Embroidery, by A. F. Kendrick. Charles Scribners & Sons. New York

The Craft of Embroidery, by Allison Liley. Mills & Boon Ltd. London

Needlemade Rugs, by Sibyl I. Mathews. Hearthside Press, Inc. New York

Samplers and Stitches, by Mrs. Archibald Christie. Hearthside Press, Inc. New York

Learning to Embroider, by Barbara Snook. Hearthside Press, Inc. New York

ABOUT THE COLOR PLATES

(All designs by the Author unless otherwise noted)

On the jacket

ROYAL JOUR—One of a series of wall hangings, this is embroidered entirely in tent stitch. Designed and worked by Everett K. Sturgeon.

I. MYTHICAL VILLAGE—Designed and worked by Mrs. John V. Kimerer. Stitches: Florentine, Gobelin, Parisian, Hungarian, Byzantine, flat, tent, rice, Scotch, jacquard, Hungarian ground, etc. Canvas work is especially adaptable to houses and buildings as texture changes can be easily rendered.

II. RECTANGLE 64—Canvas work and cut work combined. Stitches: cretan over bar filling, plain Florentine, Gobelin, buttonhole, woven cretan.

III. BURNING BUSH—21 stitches and variations: three kinds of tent, Gobelin plait, Gobelin droit, Gobelin oblique, Florentine plain, two Florentine variations, web, back, cashmere, Hungarian, two Parisian variations, satin, mosaic, bokhara, Roumanian, pattern couching, outline stitch. Diagonal tent worked from the wrong side, producing the weave effect on the front, is also incorporated.

IV. FLIGHT—Raised and padded appliqué combined with canvas work. Stitches: Gobelin, Hungarian, oblong cross, long-armed cross, turkey tufting, encroaching Gobelin, feather, chain Florentine.

V. MADONNA AND CHILD—Gobelin, Florentine, tent, bokhara couching, Hungarian, diamond trellis couching, rice, flat, Parisian and others.

INDEX

abstractionism, 79
accreditation, 103
achromatic color, 62
action school, 79
Adam furniture, 86
adapting designs, 79
"Adoration of the Magi", 14
advanced embroidery, 21
Albers, Joseph, 79
Algerian eye stitch, 36
amateur, 116
American Craftsman Council, 54
American Georgian, 86
American styles, 85
analogous color schemes, 65
appliqués, 14
asymmetrical balance, 60
awards, 114

back stitch, 48
  with oblong cross-stitch, 39
balance, 60
Bargello work, 29
basic materials, 18
basket effect, **see** plaited stitch,
  76
Bayeux tapestry, 121
Berlin wool work, 16
Bibliography, 121
binding canvas edges, 20
blackwork, 15
blocking, 88
bokhara couching, 48
Boye needles, 20
Bradford table carpet, 15
braid effect, 40
  see Vandyke stitch, 48
Buchard, Pablo, 121
buttonhole stitch, 49
Byzantine stitch, 34

Cantienti, Joseph, 121
canvas
  joining of, 91
  preparation of, 20
  selection of, 18
canvas work, definition of, 13
chain stitch, 48
chasuble, 14
chequer stitch, 32
Chippendale, 86
chroma, 62

Church Architectural Guild, 121
classes for children, 97
classification of entries, 105
classifying exhibitors, 115
closed stitch, 49
color, 51; 62
  plates described, 122
  symbolism, 81
  wheels, 63
commercial classification, 116
committees for shows, 110
complementary color schemes, 63
contrast, 58
correcting mistakes, 24
couching stitch
  bokhara, 48
  herringbone, 49
  Roumanian, 49
craft exhibitions, 115
Craft School at Penn Alps, 99
crewel work, 16
crossed corners stitch, 40
cross-stitch, 14, 27, 38
  double straight, 40
  half, 24
  Italian, 43
  long-legged, 43
  oblong, 38
  straight, 39
crossed stitches, 38
cushions, 91
cushion work, 13
cutting canvas, 47
D'Amico, Victor, 120
darning stitch, 50
Davenport, Marcia, 55
decorative arts division, 105
description of color plates, 122
design, 51
  on canvas, 68-74
  with natural forms, 76
  with stitches, 74
diagonal tent, 24
diamond eyelet stitch, 36
diaper patterns, 36
direct sketching method, 74
dominance, 56
double cross-stitch, 39
double mesh, 18
double stitch, 40
double straight cross-stitch, 40
double thread, 18

Early American, 85
ecclesiastical division, 105
ecclesiastical embroidery, 14, 18, 81
edge, binding of, 20
eighteenth century, 17
embroidery shops, 102
embroidery technician, 116
Empire period, 87
English styles, 86
English tradition, 14
equipment for teachers, 99
exhibition, 104, 115
exhibitor, how to be good, 115
eyelet stitch, see diamond eyelet, 36

façon d'Angleterre, 14
Federal Empire, 86
fern stitch, 46
filofloss, 21
filoselle, 21
fine canvas, needles for, 20
fine work, 20
finishing details, 88
fishbone stitch, 43
fish scale effect, see Florentine stitch
flame stitch, 29
flat stitch, 24, 31
Florentine stitch, 29
folded paper method, 68
frame, 20
French Provincial, 87
French stitch, 46
French styles, 87
fur effect, see tufting, Turkey knot

Georgian, 86
Gifford carpet, 15
Gobelin, 22, 24
   droit, 25
   encroaching, 27
   oblique, 27
   plait, 27, 43
   slanting, 27
graph paper method, 67
gros point, 22, 38

Harbeson, Georgiana Brown, 120
harmonies from color wheels, 63
Hatton garden hangings, 15
Hepplewhite, 86
heraldic embroidery, 81
history of embroidery, 13

household arts division, 105
hue, 62
Hungarian ground stitch, 30
Hungarian stitch, 29

impressionistic design, 76
Italian cross-stitch, 43

Jacobean work, 16
jacquard stitch, 34
Johnstone, Mildred T., 121
joining canvas, 92
judges, selection of, 107
judging, 106

Karasz, Mariska, 120
knotted stitch, 43
knitting stitch, 34
knitting yarns, 21

large cross, 40
lighting, 108
London City Guilds, 95, 103
long-armed cross, 14
long-legged cross stitch, 43

materials, 21
mercerized silk, 21
mesh, 18
Mexican, 85
mistakes, correction of, 24
moorish stitch, 33
monochromatic color scheme, 65
mosaic stitch, 31
mounting, 89-91
   cushions, 91

National Cathedral, 83
natural forms, 76
needlepoint, 21
   stitch, 24
needles, 20
needlework shows, 104
neutral color, 62
nylon sock-and-sweater yarn, 21

oblong cross-stitch, 38, 39
Opus Anglicanum, 14
Opus Pulvinarium, 13
oriental stitch, 34
orphrey, 14

painted canvases, 17
Parisian stitch, 27
pattern darning, 50
Penelope canvas mesh, 18
Pennsylvania Dutch, 85

Peri, Evi, 120
period decoration, 84
Persian yarns, 21
personal accessories, 105
petit point stitch, 24
Picasso, 79, 121
picture mounting, 89
Point d'Hungrie, 29
point scoring, 107
practicing stitches, 22
preparing the canvas, 21
primary colors, 62
principles of design, 55
professional embroiderer, 117
professional group, 116
proportion, 56
putting design on canvas, 68-74

quick-point canvas, 18
quick point, needles for, 40
quilted effect, see flat stitch, 31

raffia, 21
regency, 87
rhythm, 58
ribbons, 114
rice stitch, 40
rococo stitch, 46
    cutting canvas for, 47
Roumanian couching, 49
Royal School of Needlework, 94
rug mounting, 89
rugs
    canvas for, 20
    knitting stitch for, 34
    stitch for, 24
    Turkey knot tufting for, 46

samplers, 15, 22
scale, 56
scale of points, 107
Scotch stitch, 33
secondary colors, 62
selecting judges, 107
selling entries, 115
shapes, 79
shell stitch, 44
Sheraton, 86
show themes, 111
silk thread, 14
single mesh, 18
single thread, 18
small chequer stitch, 32
Smyrna cross, 39

Spanish, 85
standards for shows, 104
star stitch, 36
staging, 107
stem stitch, 40
stitches, 23-50
    correcting mistakes in, 24
    crossed, 38
    flat, 24
    how to design with, 74
    practicing of, 22
    procedure for practicing, 22
    vocabulary of, 23
straight cross, 39, 40
stump work, 15
symmetrical balance, 60
Syon Cope, 14

tapestry, 13, 22
    needles, 20
    wools, 21
teachers
    recommended requirements for,
        94
teaching aids, 101
tent stitch, 14, 24
    diagonal, 24
    No. 1, 24
    reverse, 24
    straight, 24
tertiary colors, 62
therapy, 99
threads, 21
tracing designs, 74
trame, 24
Tudor period, 15
tufting, Turkey knot, 15, 44, 46
    needles for, 20

unity, 55
upholstery
    needles for, 20
    stitch for, 24, 29

Vandyke stitch, 48
variety in design, 58
Victorian, 86
vocabulary of stitches, 23
Von Dommelen, David, 120

washing, 88
web stitch, 43

yarns, 21